ROCKS, FOSSILS
& GEMS

DK

A DK PUBLISHING BOOK

Project editors Janice Lacock, Louise Pritchard
Art editors Alison Anholt-White,
Neville Graham, Thomas Keene
Managing editor Gillian Denton
Managing art editor Julia Harris
Production Louise Barratt
Picture research Cynthia Hole, Kathy Lockley
Consultants Dr. R.F. Symes (Natural History Museum,
London), Dr. Wendy Kirk (University College, London)

First American Edition, 1997
2 4 6 8 10 9 7 5 3 1

Published in the United States by
DK Publishing, Inc., 95 Madison Avenue
New York, New York 10016

Visit us on the World Wide Web at http://www.dk.com

ISBN 0-7894-2219-0

Reproduced in Singapore by Colourscan.
Printed in Singapore by Toppan.

Rock containing
tourmaline,
quartz, and
albite crystals

Aphthitalite

Golden topaz crystal

A 19th-century
gold box with
rare gems

Skull of Jurassic ichthyosaur

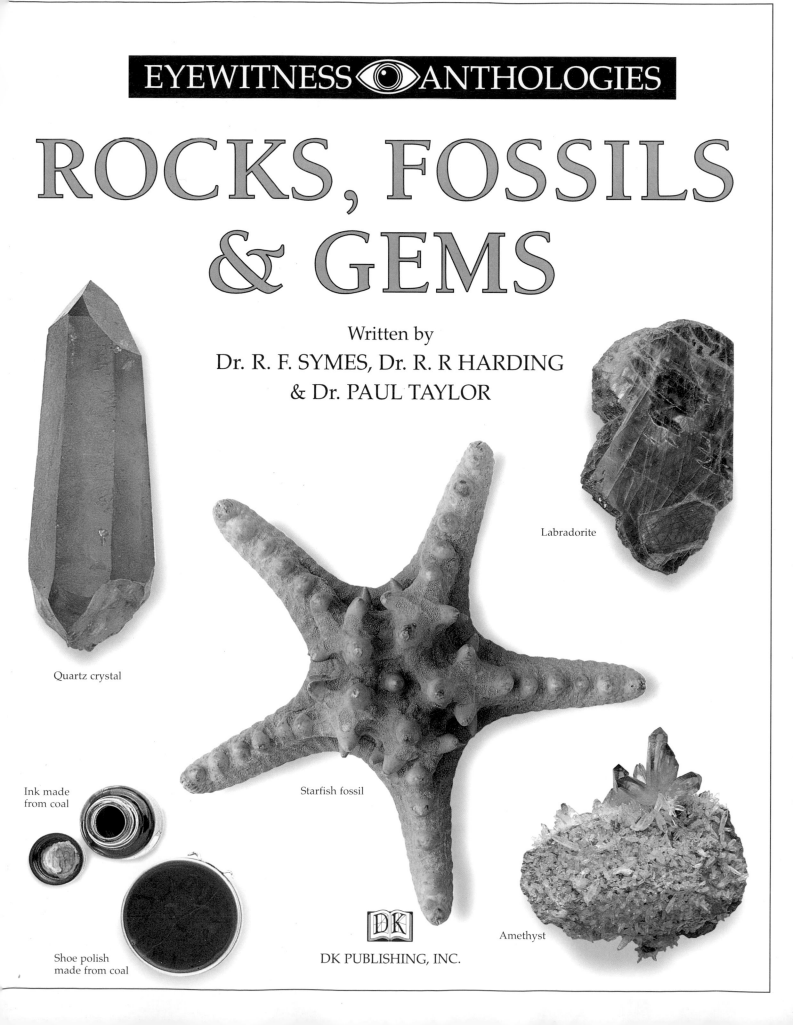

EYEWITNESS ANTHOLOGIES

ROCKS, FOSSILS & GEMS

Written by
Dr. R. F. SYMES, Dr. R. R HARDING
& Dr. PAUL TAYLOR

Labradorite

Quartz crystal

Starfish fossil

Ink made
from coal

Amethyst

Shoe polish
made from coal

DK

DK PUBLISHING, INC.

Contents

Introduction

This book has been designed to show the great diversity and wealth of materials below the Earth's surface – from fossils, to rocks and minerals, and crystals and gems. The first section (pp. 6–43) concentrates on the fossilized remains of various creatures that lived millions of years ago. The second section (pp. 44–75) explains how rocks (in particular, igneous, volcanic, sedimentary, and metamorphic) are formed and where they are found, and examines precious metals such as silver and gold. The third section (pp. 76–125) dwells on the world's exquisite crystals and gems (especially diamond, quartz, corundum, beryl, and opal), and looks at the use of crystals in the home.

Brightly colored *Haliotis* shell

Fossil *Turritella*

Modern sea lily fossil

Cut aquamarine

The changing world

THE HISTORY OF LIFE has been played out on a world that has been changing constantly since it was formed about 4,600 million years ago (mya). The Earth's crust is divided into several plates which move relative to one another. Most earthquakes and volcanoes occur along boundaries between these plates. The combined effects of many small plate movements have caused continents to drift across the Earth, to collide and form mountains, and to break into pieces. Continents are still moving today. North America is separating from Europe at a rate of about 0.8 in (2 cm) per year. Sea levels and climates have changed many times. This is why fossils of sea creatures can be found inland, and why fossils of tropical plants can be found where the climate is cold. The maps on these pages show the shape of the land at four stages in geological history. The fossils show a selection of the life that existed during each different time span, and many are featured later in this book.

CONTINUOUS CHANGE
Earthquakes such as the great one of Lisbon, Portugal, in 1755 (above), and the one that devastated Armenia, U.S.S.R., in 1988 show that changes are still taking place on Earth.

Carboniferous mollusk (bellerophontid)

Carboniferous coral

Devonian fish

Carboniferous seed fern

THE OLDEST FOSSILS
The world's oldest fossils are tiny bacteria-like cells 3,500 million years old. Complex animals made of many cells, like this *Tribrachidium* from Australia, appeared at the end of the Precambrian.

Silurian trilobites

Silurian graptolites

Silurian gastropod

Silurian brachiopods

Carboniferous crinoid

EARLY PALEOZOIC WORLD (409–590 MYA)
Paleozoic means "ancient life." During the early Paleozoic Era (Cambrian, Ordovician, and Silurian Periods, p. 9), a large continent, known as Gondwanaland, was situated over the southern polar region. Most early Paleozoic life was in the sea. Invertebrates (animals without backbones) were especially numerous, but primitive fishes were also present. Plants began to live on land toward the end of this time.

Gondwanaland

LATE PALEOZOIC WORLD (249–408 MYA)
Life diversified greatly during the late Paleozoic Era (Devonian, Carboniferous, and Permian Periods), at the end of which most of the land was joined in one supercontinent known as Pangea. Amphibians, reptiles, insects, and other animals colonized the land where they could feed on the vegetation that had developed. A mass extinction of much of the life occurred at the very end of the Paleozoic.

Pangea

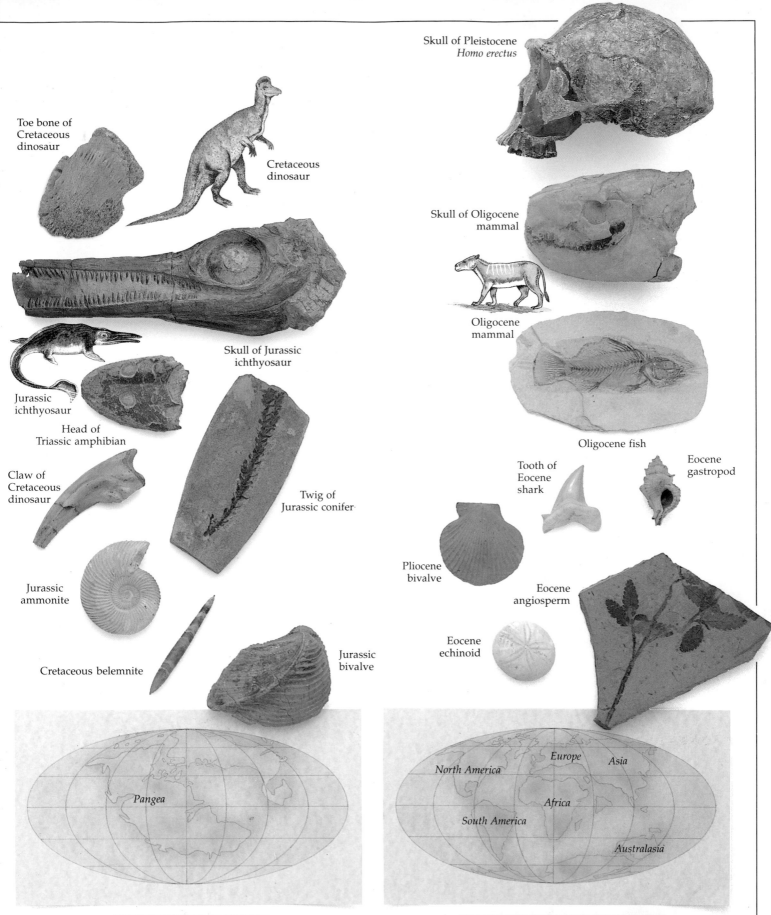

Toe bone of
Cretaceous
dinosaur

Cretaceous
dinosaur

Skull of Pleistocene
Homo erectus

Skull of Oligocene
mammal

Oligocene
mammal

Skull of Jurassic
ichthyosaur

Jurassic
ichthyosaur

Head of
Triassic amphibian

Oligocene fish

Claw of
Cretaceous
dinosaur

Tooth of
Eocene
shark

Eocene
gastropod

Twig of
Jurassic conifer

Pliocene
bivalve

Eocene
angiosperm

Jurassic
ammonite

Eocene
echinoid

Cretaceous belemnite

Jurassic
bivalve

Pangea

Europe   *Asia*

North America

Africa

South America

Australasia

MESOZOIC WORLD (66–248 MYA)
Mesozoic means "middle life." The Mesozoic Era (Cretaceous, Jurassic,
and Triassic periods) is known as the Age of Reptiles. Dinosaurs stalked
the land, pterosaurs swooped through the sky, and ichthyosaurs swam in
the sea with belemnites and ammonites. Flowering plants and small
mammals appeared, Pangea began to break up, and many species were
wiped out in another mass extinction at the end of the Mesozoic.

CENOZOIC WORLD (PRESENT DAY–65 MYA)
The world as we know it gradually took shape during the Cenozoic Era
(Paleocene to Holocene epochs). Cenozoic means "recent life." India moved
northward and collided with Asia, forming the Himalayas. Mammals and
flowering plants became more varied and dominant on land; teleosts (a
group of bony fishes) and sea urchins were among groups abundant in the
sea. Our own genus, *Homo*, appeared in the Pleistocene.

The making of rocks

THE MANY KINDS OF ROCKS beneath our feet have been forming for more than 4,000 million years. The Earth's crust is made up of elements. The important ones are oxygen, silicon, aluminum, iron, calcium, sodium, potassium, magnesium, and carbon. These combine in different ways to form minerals. All rocks are made up of minerals. Common rock-forming minerals include calcite (calcium carbonate), quartz (silicon dioxide), and feldspars (complex minerals containing aluminum, silicon, calcium, sodium, and potassium). There are three groups of rocks: igneous, metamorphic, and sedimentary.

AMETHYST
This is the purple variety of the mineral quartz. If allowed to grow freely, quartz crystals are pointed and hexagonal (six-sided).

FOLDED ROCK
Powerful movements in the Earth's crust can cause rocks to crack and form faults, or to buckle, creating folds like this.

Distorted trilobite

TWISTED TRILOBITE
Metamorphic rocks may contain distorted fossils such as this trilobite (p. 30) in slate.

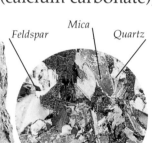

Feldspar   *Mica*   *Quartz*

Black mica
Glassy quartz
White feldspar

Thin section of granite

GRANITE
The speckles in this granite are individual minerals. Granite is an igneous rock formed at great depths.

Molten rocks

Igneous rocks are formed by the cooling of molten magma (liquid rock) from deep within the Earth. Sometimes the magma reaches the surface and erupts from volcanoes as lava before it cools. Most often, though, the magma cools and becomes solid deep underground.

LAYER UPON LAYER
The Grand Canyon in Arizona, formed by the erosion of sandstone and limestone, is a natural slice through the Earth's crust. The oldest stratum, or layer, is at the bottom, the youngest at the top.

Band rich in mica

Band rich in quartz

SCHIST
Parallel banding of minerals is a common feature of metamorphic rocks. Schist is formed from shale or mud.

Changed rocks

High temperatures and pressures can change rocks into new types called metamorphic rocks. Marble is a metamorphosed limestone; slate, a metamorphosed shale.

Band of quartz

Band of silicate minerals

Thin section of schist

One varve

Fine sediment
Coarse sediment

ROCK BANDS
Stratification on a much smaller scale than the Grand Canyon is seen in this sedimentary rock. Each set of one light layer (fine sediment) and one dark layer (coarse sediment) is a year's accumulation of silt and mud, called a varve, at the bottom of a glacier-fed lake. Such well-defined seasonal bands are rare.

CHALK CLIFFS
Chalk is a pure white limestone composed mostly of the skeletons of tiny marine plants.

CONGLOMERATE
This is a coarse sedimentary rock consisting of rounded pebbles bound together by a natural mineral cement. Conglomerate can look a lot like manufactured concrete.

Pebble

Natural cement

Loose sand grains

Sandstone

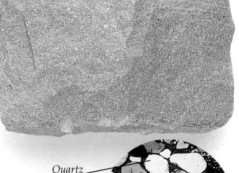

Quartz

Iron-rich cement

Thin section of sandstone

Deposited rocks

Rocks are continually being eroded, creating grains which are carried by rivers, by the sea, and by the wind. These grains are deposited, together with the remains of animals and plants, as mud, sand, or coarser material. As this sediment is buried deeper by more sediment, it is compacted (pressed down) and cemented by the growth of minerals to form a sedimentary rock. Sandstone, for example, is a sedimentary rock made from cemented sand.

FROM ROCK TO ROCK
As cliffs of sedimentary rocks are eroded, small pieces of rock are deposited on the beach. These will be eroded further and may eventually form new sedimentary rock.

Shell fragment

Thin section of limestone

Finely broken shells

FOSSIL CONTAINER
Many sedimentary rocks contain hard lumps called concretions or nodules. These were formed after the sediment was deposited, often around fossil shells like this clam (pp. 18–19).

Clam shell

FOSSILIFEROUS ROCK
Limestone is a sedimentary rock composed mainly of calcite and a few other similar carbonate minerals. The calcite is usually derived from the broken shells and skeletons of animals and plants that lived in the sea. Larger, more intact shells can also be present, and limestones are therefore good rocks in which to hunt for fossils. This Silurian limestone contains some fossil brachiopods (pp. 16–17).

Fossil brachiopod

Era	Period	Million years ago (mya)
Cenozoic	Holocene (epoch)	0.01
	Pleistocene (epoch)	2
	Pliocene (epoch)	5
	Miocene (epoch)	25
	Oligocene (epoch)	38
	Eocene (epoch)	55
	Paleocene (epoch)	65
Mesozoic	Cretaceous	144
	Jurassic	213
	Triassic	248
Paleozoic	Permian	286
	Carboniferous	360
	Devonian	408
	Silurian	438
	Ordovician	505
	Cambrian	590
	Precambrian (about seven times longer than all the other periods put together)	4,600 (origin of the Earth)

STRATIGRAPHICAL COLUMN
A series of eras and periods (and epochs in the Cenozoic) are used to describe the age of rocks and fossils.

Early paleontology

The frontispiece to the museum catalog of the naturalist Johann Scheuchzer (1672–1733)

THE SERIOUS SCIENTIFIC STUDY OF FOSSILS began only about 300 years ago, although early Greek philosophers such as Pythagoras are reported to have realized the true nature of fossils as long ago as the 5th century B.C. During the Middle Ages in Europe (A.D. 400-1400), many naturalists thought fossils were the products of a mysterious "plastic force" ("*vis plastica*") which formed the fossils within the Earth. Their true origin as the buried remains of ancient animals and plants was established beyond reasonable doubt by Steno (see below) and other naturalists of the 17th century. Fossils were subsequently used to solve geological problems such as the relative ages of different rocks, and also biological problems concerning the evolution and the origin and extinction of various forms of life on Earth. Today scientists throughout the world are still studying fossils, and our understanding of them is increasing all the time.

NOAH'S ARK
The Bible story of Noah tells how he took animals onto his ark to escape the great flood. Many naturalists, including Steno, believed that the Biblical Flood had transported and buried fossils. This explained why fossil sea shells occurred on mountaintops. (Scheuchzer once identified the fossil of a salamander as the skeleton of a human drowned in the Flood!)

TONGUE STONES
Fossil shark teeth from Cenozoic rocks around the Mediterranean were known to naturalists as tongue stones. Some naturalists believed that they grew naturally within the rocks, but Steno and others realized their correct origins.

STENO
Niels Stensen (1638-1686), better known as Steno, was a Dane who worked as the court physician at Florence in Italy. He was one of the first people to realize the true nature of fossils, when in 1667, he noticed that the teeth of a stranded shark were very similar to tongue stones.

RESTORATION OF *PALAEOTHERIUM*
Cuvier studied *Palaeotherium* bones from the Eocene rocks of Montmartre in Paris. The animal from which they came was restored as this tapir-like mammal.

Grinding teeth of a herbivore

GEORGES CUVIER
The French naturalist Georges Cuvier (1769–1832) made many important contributions to natural history. Early in his scientific career he realized that the different parts of an animal's body were closely interrelated; for example, mammals with horns and hoofs were all herbivores (plant eaters) and would have had the teeth of herbivores. The significance of this observation was that entire animals could now be restored – shown as they would have looked when alive – from the evidence of isolated bones. Cuvier also recognized that many fossils belonged to extinct species, and he devised a view of Earth history in which a succession of catastrophes exterminated earlier forms of life. According to Cuvier, the last of these catastrophes was the Biblical Flood.

Fossil jaw of *Palaeotherium*

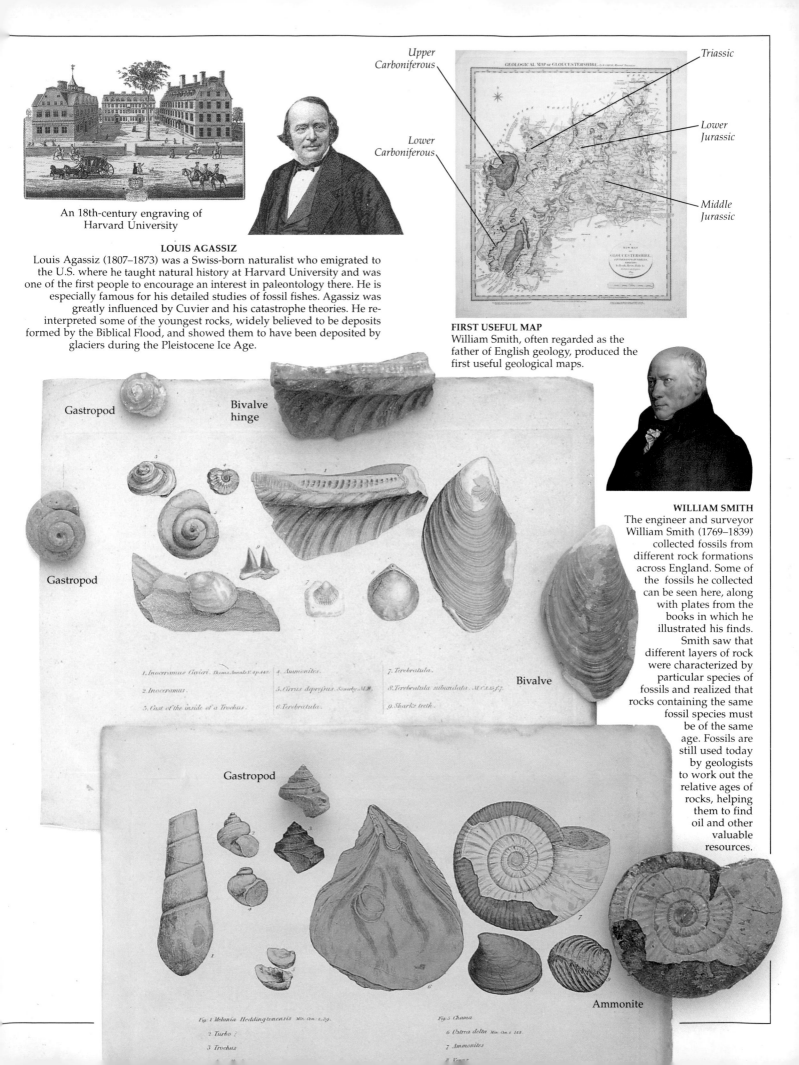

An 18th-century engraving of
Harvard University

Upper
Carboniferous

Triassic

Lower
Jurassic

Lower
Carboniferous

Middle
Jurassic

LOUIS AGASSIZ

Louis Agassiz (1807–1873) was a Swiss-born naturalist who emigrated to
the U.S. where he taught natural history at Harvard University and was
one of the first people to encourage an interest in paleontology there. He is
especially famous for his detailed studies of fossil fishes. Agassiz was
greatly influenced by Cuvier and his catastrophe theories. He re-
interpreted some of the youngest rocks, widely believed to be deposits
formed by the Biblical Flood, and showed them to have been deposited by
glaciers during the Pleistocene Ice Age.

FIRST USEFUL MAP

William Smith, often regarded as the
father of English geology, produced the
first useful geological maps.

Gastropod

Bivalve
hinge

Gastropod

Gastropod

WILLIAM SMITH

The engineer and surveyor
William Smith (1769–1839)
collected fossils from
different rock formations
across England. Some of
the fossils he collected
can be seen here, along
with plates from the
books in which he
illustrated his finds.
Smith saw that
different layers of rock
were characterized by
particular species of
fossils and realized that
rocks containing the same
fossil species must
be of the same
age. Fossils are
still used today
by geologists
to work out the
relative ages of
rocks, helping
them to find
oil and other
valuable
resources.

1. *Inoceramus Cuvieri. Thoms. Annals V. 4 p. 448.*
2. *Inoceramus.*
3. *Cast of the inside of a Trochus.*
4. *Ammonites.*
5. *Cirrus depressus. Sowerby. M.S.*
6. *Terebratula.*
7. *Terebratula.*
8. *Terebratula subundata. M.C.t.15.f.7.*
9. *Sharks teeth.*

Bivalve

Ammonite

Fig. 1 Melania Heddingtonensis Min. Con. t. 39.
2 Turbo ?
3 Trochus

Fig. 5 Chama
6 Ostrea delta Min. Con. t. 148.
7 Ammonites

Remarkable remains

Skin traces

Part   Counterpart

FOSSILS OF SOFT TISSUES, which usually decay during fossilization, are sometimes found. These include entirely soft-bodied animals which are otherwise unrepresented in the fossil record. Fossilization of soft parts is of great importance because it supplies much more information about the living animals than do bones, teeth, or shells. Discoveries of preserved humans are always exciting and include those at Pompeii in Italy and Grauballe in Denmark.

IN TWO PARTS
The outline of the body is clearly shown in this fossilized frog. Even traces of the skin and other fleshy tissues have been preserved. The rock has split straight through the preserved animal, leaving the fossil in two pieces known as the part and counterpart.

STICKY DEATH
A spider can clearly be seen in this piece of amber, the fossilized resin of an ancient plant. Amber often contains animals that were trapped in the sticky resin as it dripped down trunks and stems. Insects, spiders, and even small lizards and frogs have been preserved for millions of years in this way.

UNIQUE INFORMATION
This unusual worm is from a deposit known as the Burgess Shale in British Columbia, Canada, famous for its soft-bodied fossils. Other animals discovered in the Burgess Shale include trilobites (pp. 22–23) with their limbs intact, primitive crustaceans, and several bizarre creatures that do not fit within any groups living today. These animals were buried in mudflows on the Cambrian sea bed over 500 million years ago, and their fossils provide us with a unique glimpse of a very varied early community.

EXCEPTIONAL INSECT
This delicate dragonfly was buried in mud which formed the Solnhofen Limestone of Bavaria, West Germany, a deposit renowned for its exceptional fossils.

DEEP-FROZEN MAMMOTH
Mammoths have occasionally been recovered from the permafrost (permanently frozen ground) of Siberia, northern Asia. They were probably trapped and frozen when they fell into cracks in glaciers. Mammoths lived during the Ice Ages of the last two million years and became extinct about 12,000 years ago. The largest species grew to over 13 ft (4 m) at the shoulder.

ACTIVE VOLCANO
The famous volcano Vesuvius in southeast Italy has erupted frequently over the years. It has been quiet since 1944 but is not thought to be extinct.

Cast of body from Pompeii

BURIED IN ASH
During the violent eruption of Mount Vesuvius in A.D. 79, inhabitants of the nearby towns of Pompeii and Herculaneum were buried beneath avalanches of volcanic ash and debris. The bodies lasted long enough for the ash to harden around them, and when they decayed they left cavities. The cavities were excavated and then filled with plaster to make casts, which gruesomely revealed victims' postures at the moment of death. Some bodies of pets have also been found.

SOFT PRESERVATION *left*

Belemnoteuthis from the Jurassic is related to squid, cuttlefish, and the extinct belemnites (pp. 20–21). The internal skeleton of this specimen is hidden beneath the soft body, which has been preserved because of replacement by the mineral apatite soon after death and burial. Even the hooked tentacles around the head can be seen. Ink was released from a sac as a defensive screen, an ability that *Belemnoteuthis*'s relatives possess today.

Hooked tentacles

Preserved soft body hides the internal skeleton

The cast of the body shows exactly how this person was lying when he was buried by ash over 1,900 years ago

Bone

Skin

Fossil moa foot

SKINNY CLAW

The moas of New Zealand were large flightless birds related to the kiwi, emu, and ostrich. The biggest was 11 ft (3.5 m) tall. Although now extinct, moas were alive when Maoris first lived in New Zealand 700 years ago. Fossils of many different species of moa have been found, some over two million years old. This fossilized foot still has skin attached. The impact these once dominant birds had on New Zealand's native vegetation is still evident today in plants that have evolved a resistance to being eaten by moas!

Claw

A moa among kiwis

Reconstruction of a mammoth stuck in the tar at La Brea

STUCK FAST

Tar oozing naturally to the surface at La Brea in Los Angeles, California, has entombed many animals accidentally caught in the sticky substance over the past 10,000 to 20,000 years. Excavations in the older solidified layers of tar have unearthed the bones of extinct mammals such as mammoths and saber-toothed cats.

GRAUBALLE MAN

Human bodies in remarkable states of preservation have been excavated from several peat bogs in northern Europe. The acid material of the bogs prevented the total decay of soft parts. Many bodies are over 2,000 years old, and some show signs of a ritual killing. This man was found in 1952 near the village of Grauballe in Denmark. He died in about the 4th century. Skin and internal organs – even re- mains of his last meal – have been preserved.

Corals

CORALS ARE SOME OF THE MOST BEAUTIFUL ANIMALS in the sea. The colorful massed tentacles of coral individuals, or polyps, resemble flowers in an undersea garden. Most corals live in warm, shallow, tropical waters and feed on plankton but also obtain nutrition from algae which may live within their bodies. Corals may be solitary (living by themselves) or colonial (many polyps joined together). Fossil corals are common because beneath the soft-bodied polyps are hard, chalky skeletons. The oldest are from the Ordovician. Related sea anemones and jellyfish lack hard skeletons and are seldom fossilized.

CORAL FISHING
Coral has long been collected for its beauty and is used in jewelry.

A ring-shaped coral reef is called an atoll

Individual coral skeleton

Separate corallite

Red limestone

PIPE CORAL
This is a colony of *Acrocyathus*, a Carboniferous coral. The pipe-shaped corallites (skeletons formed by individual polyps) grew separately. The spaces between them are now filled with red limestone.

HORN CORAL
Aulophyllum, shown here in two pieces, is a typical solitary coral. It lived on the sea bed, growing in this characteristic horn shape. The pointed end was buried in sediment on the sea bed, and the soft polyp sat on top of the other end.

PACKED COLONY
Lonsdaleia is a colonial coral which belongs to a group called the Rugosa. Rugose corals became extinct in the Permian. The individual corallites which make up the colony are many-sided, usually hexagonal (six-sided), because they are so tightly packed together.

MODERN CORALS
Most modern corals belong to a group called the scleractinians which first appeared in the Triassic. Coral reefs are inhabited by countless numbers of different animals and are the most diverse marine environments.

Pale sediment filling areas once occupied by soft tissues

CHAIN CORAL
The corallites of the Silurian coral *Halysites* are arranged in long branching ribbons. On the surface, the coral looks like a collection of chains.

BRAIN CORAL
Together, the individuals of brain corals form winding valleys, and the colonies resemble human brains. Polyps may share a common mouth with others in the same valley. This Miocene example has been cut horizontally and polished to show the inside.

Winding valley of coral

Branch of corallites

RECORD-BREAKING CORAL
This fossilized fragment is of the reef-building coral *Galaxea*. The structure of the individual skeletons can easily be seen. The world's largest known living coral is a *Galaxea* colony from Okinawa in Japan. It has a circumference (outer boundary) of 52 ft (16 m).

Individual coral skeleton

CORAL BUSH
Colonies of the coral *Thamnopora* are bush-shaped, with corallites opening all over the surfaces of the branches. This example is in a piece of limestone which has been cut across horizontally and polished to show the shape of the colony.

Fossil *Fungia*

SOLITARY CORALS
These unusual-looking fossils are the delicate skeletons of the solitary corals *Stephanophyllia* and *Fungia*, which lived on the sea bed in the Pliocene and Pleistocene respectively. As their name suggests, the skeletons of *Fungia* look like the undersides of mushrooms.

Fossil *Stephanophyllia*

REPLACED CORAL
The skeletons of some fossil corals are made of the mineral aragonite. Aragonite dissolves easily, so the skeletons often disappear during fossilization. In this fossil colony of *Thecosmilia* the skeletons have been replaced by silica.

Skeleton replaced by silica

Sea bed dwellers

CLOSE NEIGHBORS
Bryozoan colonies can be compared to blocks of apartments and other buildings containing several similar homes.

Aᴍᴏɴɢ ᴛʜᴇ ᴍᴏꜱᴛ ᴄᴏᴍᴍᴏɴ ꜰᴏꜱꜱɪʟꜱ to be found are the remains of animals and plants which lived on the sea bed. They lived where sand and mud were regularly deposited, and most of the animals had hard parts which could survive decay and be fossilized. The plants and many of the animals could not escape burial, even when they were alive, because they lacked the ability to move. Bryozoans and brachiopods are living examples of this type of animal but because they live in the sea, many people are not aware of their existence. Today, there are only 250 known species of brachiopods. This contrasts with the huge numbers – about 30,000 – of known fossil species.

Holes in the colony through which water and food particles are pumped

ARCHIMEDES' SCREW
This distinctive Carboniferous bryozoan is named after a spiral water pump invented by the Greek mathematician Archimedes. The screw-shaped skeleton once supported a twisted net of individuals similar to *Hornera* (center left).

Archimedes' water pump

Each piece is a colony containing at least 200 individuals

Free-living colonies of Cretaceous bryozoans

COMMUNITY HOMES *above*
Because of their branching shape, this type of modern bryozoan, *Hornera*, often provides a home for worms, small fishes, and many other animals in the sea.

One individual skeleton

Calcite colonies

Bryozoans are tiny animals which live in colonies where each individual is attached to its neighbor. A colony may contain tens, hundreds, or even thousands of individuals, each one less than 0.04 in (1 mm) long. They have tentacles which they use to feed on tiny particles of food. Most have calcite skeletons. Colonies, which grow by budding new individuals, vary in shape. Some are flat sheets; others grow upright and look like nets or bushes.

Light and dark growth bands

LARGER THAN LIFE
The calcite skeletons of individuals in a bryozoan colony are magnified here many times.

OLD LACE
The fragments of lace bryozoan (*Chasmatopora*) in this Ordovician shale are among the oldest known bryozoans.

BEETROOT STONE
The red color of the Jurassic alga *Solenopora* is sometimes preserved, and these fossils are then known as beetroot stones.

Shells on stalks

Brachiopods have two shells and can be confused with bivalve mollusks (pp. 18–19). The soft parts of bivalve mollusks are very different, though, and the two types of shell can be distinguished in most cases. A brachiopod shell is symmetrical (even) but one of the pair is larger than the other. A bivalve shell is asymmetrical (uneven) but is a mirror image of its pair. Brachiopods may have a hole at one end for the pedicle, or stalk, which the animals used to attach themselves to hard surfaces when they were alive.

Hole for stalk

Fossil brachiopod

Hole for wick

Roman lamp

Hole for stalk

Modern brachiopods

Symmetrical shell

WINGED SHELLS
Spiriferid brachiopods had an internal spiral-shaped feeding organ, supported by a fragile skeleton.

Larger shell

Spiriferid brachiopods

Side view of Cretaceous brachiopod

Nummulite skeleton in limestone block

LAMP SHELLS
Brachiopods are known popularly as lamp shells because some look similar to ancient Roman lamps. The hole at one end of the lamp for a wick is matched by the hole in the brachiopod shell which was for its stalk.

TODAY'S COLOR
These red brachiopods of today are very similar to the Cretaceous one which has lost any color it might have had during fossilization.

Modern branching sponge

Polished fossil *Siphonia* sponge

PYRAMID SKELETONS
The pyramids of Giza in Egypt are built of blocks of limestone made up of skeletons like those of the single-celled animal *Nummulites*.

Sponges

Sponges are a primitive group of animals which pump water through their bodies and take food particles from it. Sponges have skeletons made up of small spicules which can often be fossilized. The first fossil sponges occur as long ago as the Cambrian.

Fossil tulip sponge

Pyramids built for the pharaohs of ancient Egypt

SKELETON CUP
Skeletons of sponges with fused spicules can occasionally be preserved intact. Many are cup-shaped like this Cretaceous example.

Sponge skeleton treated to make a bath sponge

Shells of all shapes

AT THE BEGINNING of the Cambrian period, about 550 million years ago, complex animals with hard shells and skeletons first appeared in the sea. Among these were the mollusks, a group of animals which are still abundant today. Gastropods, or snails, and bivalves such as clams, mussels, and oysters, are the best-known mollusks; other kinds include chitons and cephalopods (pp. 20–21). Bivalves have two shells, or valves, joined together by a hinge. Gastropods have only one shell. The shells of mollusks are often found as fossils. Most are made of calcite, or of aragonite which dissolves more easily. Internal molds of mollusks are often found because aragonite shells may become filled with sediment and the shells themselves dissolved.

VENUS'S SHELL
The Roman goddess Venus emerging from a scallop shell.

ANCIENT JEWELS
This mudstone contains rare fossil pearls. They are from the Eocene, and are about 50 million years old.

Pearl

Hinge tooth

Muscle scar

HINGED TOGETHER
Hinge teeth help hold a bivalve's shells together when it is alive. This shell belonged to an Eocene bivalve, *Venericardia*.

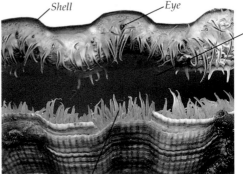

Shell

Eye

Gape

Sensory tentacles

GOOD EYESIGHT
Scallops have many eyes, each of which has well-developed focusing lenses. The eyes are situated in soft tissue near the edge of the shells, which are hinged together. To feed, scallops open their shells and use their gills to force a current of water, laden with food particles, through the "gape" in the shells.

SPINES FOR SPONGES
The "thorny oyster" *Spondylus* is so named because of its spiny shell, as seen in this Pliocene specimen. Spines of modern *Spondylus* help sponges and other encrusting animals grow on their shells, which protects the bivalve from predators.

Prominent rib

FALLING APART
These fossilized shells, one flat, the other convex (domed), belong to the scallop *Pecten* from the Pliocene. The prominent ribs on the two shells interlock, but, as with many bivalve fossils, the shells are usually found separated because the connecting ligament rots away.

CARVED IN STONE
An ancient Arabic prayer has been carved on these two fossils. They are internal casts of bivalves (pp. 24–25) formed by sediment which solidified in the space between the shells.

Modern snail shell

Fossil snail shells

DISAPPEARING COLOR
Some living gastropods, especially those of the tropics, are often brightly colored because of chemical substances within the shell called pigments. Unfortunately, pigments are usually destroyed during fossilization.

Modern Cone shell

Fossil Cone shell

Siphon

Foot

SOFT-HEARTED
This present-day sea snail is just emerging from its shell. Parts of its soft body can clearly be seen (at top and bottom right).

Modern snail

Curious coils

Gastropod shells of all ages come in many different shapes and sizes. They are all open at one end and are usually twisted into a spiral coil with a gradually increasing diameter. The exact shape of the spiral varies according to the species. It can be left-handed, right-handed, loosely coiled or tightly coiled, regular or irregular. The coiling of the shell on the freshwater snail *Planorbis* is almost flat. The shell of *Turritella* is drawn out into a high spire.

Spiral coil

Fossil *Turritella*

"WORM SHELLS"
Vermetids are unusual for gastropods as they attach themselves permanently to a hard surface, often in clusters like these fossil examples. Their shells are irregularly coiled and look more like worms.

Fossil chiton

Modern chiton

NO CONNECTION
Chitons are a small group of marine mollusks with shells made up of eight individual plates. Fossil chitons are rare and their plates are disconnected. Today, chitons can be found in tide pools, clinging to the sides of the rocks from which they scrape algae for food.

LOOSE COILS
Tubina is a very unusual type of mollusk which belonged to a now-extinct group called the bellerophontids. It has a loosely coiled shell and dates from the Devonian Period. It is uncertain whether *Tubina* was a true gastropod or not because its soft body has not been preserved.

Left-handed coil

Right-handed coil

SPIRAL FOSSILS
Most gastropod shells have a right-handed spiral coil, such as *Neptunea despecta*. The shell of *Neptunea contraria* has a left-handed coil.

Fossil *Neptunea contraria*

Fossil *Neptunea despecta*

Siphonal canal

EXTRA LONG
The pointed shell of *Fusinus* is further lengthened by a siphonal canal which the animal used in respiration.

Top

Fossil *Planorbis*

Underneath

Intelligent mollusks

An ammonite with its shell partly replaced by iron pyrites

THE OCTOPUS, SQUID, and cuttlefish are modern representatives of a group of sea-dwelling mollusks called cephalopods, which have left a rich fossil record. Cephalopods are regarded as the most highly developed mollusks. They have suckered tentacles, eyes that are remarkably similar to more advanced vertebrate animals, and the ability to learn and use their learning. They are active predators, moving quickly through the water using a type of jet propulsion. Most modern cephalopods have internal shells completely covered by soft parts. However, like the living *Nautilus*, many fossil cephalopods, including the ammonites, had external shells that were similar to the shells of snails but were divided into chambers. Following their first appearance in the Cambrian, many different species of cephalopods came and went, making them very useful fossils for dating rocks (pp. 8–9).

DECORATIVE MOTIF
The beautiful shape of ammonites is often used in decoration. This is a column from a terraced house in Brighton, England. The architect's name was Amon!

IMPORTANT EVIDENCE
As the only living nautiloid, *Nautilus* is the closest modern relative of the ammonites, and provides us with important clues about this extinct group. *Nautilus* is a nocturnal animal, active only at night, and lives in the Pacific Ocean at depths ranging from 16 to 1,800 ft (5 to 550 m). Its prey consists of fish and crustaceans which it eats with its hard beak.

Septa dividing shell into chambers

Final chamber

Complex suture line

Ammonites

VARIOUS SIZES
Some Mesozoic ammonites reached gigantic sizes. This large specimen, about 12 in (30 cm) wide, is small compared to giants which could be 6 ft (2 m) in diameter.

Simple suture line

Fossil nautiloids

ROOMS FOR EXPANSION
Fossil ammonites and nautiloids have coiled shells divided into a series of chambers by membranes called septa. Only the final chamber next to the opening was occupied by the animal. As it grew, the animal periodically moved forward and formed new septa at the rear of the body chamber. Older chambers were filled with liquid and gas, the proportions of which could be changed through a canal called the siphuncle to allow the animal to move up and down in the sea. Suture lines, formed where the septa meet the shell, are simple in nautiloids but are folded into complex saddles and lobes in ammonites.

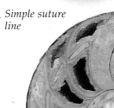

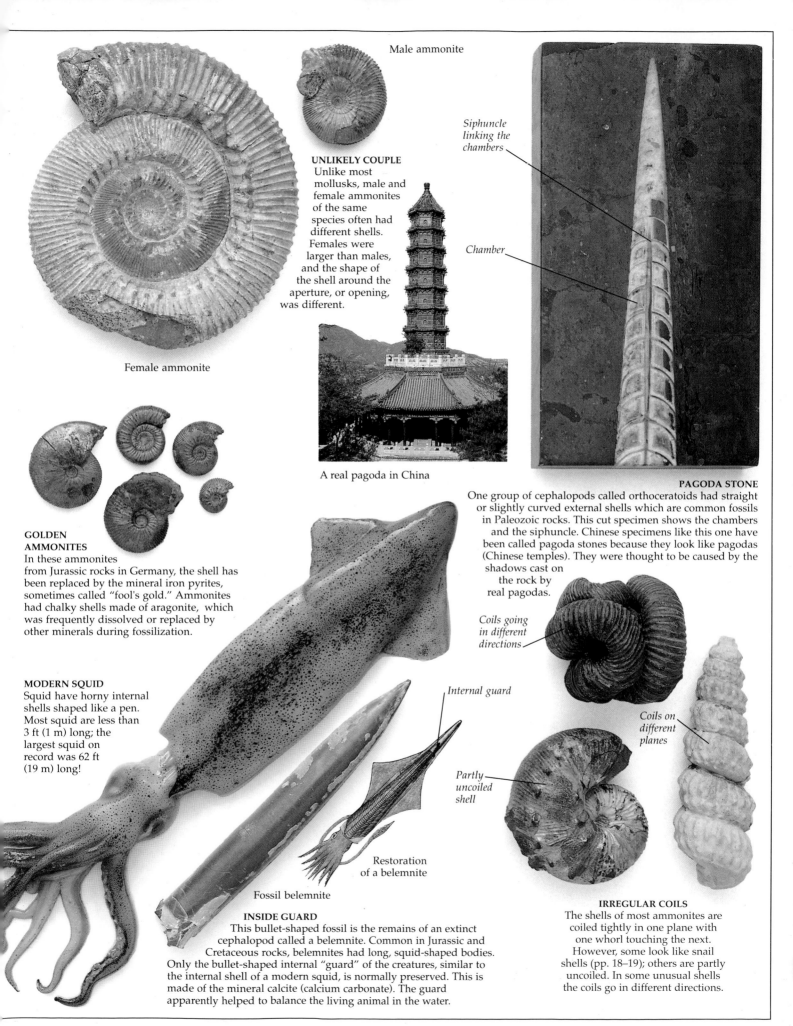

Male ammonite

Female ammonite

UNLIKELY COUPLE
Unlike most mollusks, male and female ammonites of the same species often had different shells. Females were larger than males, and the shape of the shell around the aperture, or opening, was different.

A real pagoda in China

Siphuncle linking the chambers

Chamber

PAGODA STONE
One group of cephalopods called orthoceratoids had straight or slightly curved external shells which are common fossils in Paleozoic rocks. This cut specimen shows the chambers and the siphuncle. Chinese specimens like this one have been called pagoda stones because they look like pagodas (Chinese temples). They were thought to be caused by the shadows cast on the rock by real pagodas.

GOLDEN AMMONITES
In these ammonites from Jurassic rocks in Germany, the shell has been replaced by the mineral iron pyrites, sometimes called "fool's gold." Ammonites had chalky shells made of aragonite, which was frequently dissolved or replaced by other minerals during fossilization.

MODERN SQUID
Squid have horny internal shells shaped like a pen. Most squid are less than 3 ft (1 m) long; the largest squid on record was 62 ft (19 m) long!

Internal guard

Coils going in different directions

Coils on different planes

Partly uncoiled shell

Restoration of a belemnite

Fossil belemnite

INSIDE GUARD
This bullet-shaped fossil is the remains of an extinct cephalopod called a belemnite. Common in Jurassic and Cretaceous rocks, belemnites had long, squid-shaped bodies. Only the bullet-shaped internal "guard" of the creatures, similar to the internal shell of a modern squid, is normally preserved. This is made of the mineral calcite (calcium carbonate). The guard apparently helped to balance the living animal in the water.

IRREGULAR COILS
The shells of most ammonites are coiled tightly in one plane with one whorl touching the next. However, some look like snail shells (pp. 18–19); others are partly uncoiled. In some unusual shells the coils go in different directions.

21

Animals in armor

Insects, spiders, crabs, scorpions, lobsters, millipedes, barnacles, and many other animals belong to a major group of animals called arthropods, a word which means "jointed foot." Some arthropods live in the sea, some live on land, and some fly; but very few are found as fossils. All arthropods have jointed legs, a segmented body, and an exoskeleton, or outer armor. As the animal grows, it has to shed its exoskeleton every so often and grow another one. Some arthropods – the extinct trilobites, for example – have the mineral calcite in their exoskeletons, making them resistant to decay. These exoskeletons are the parts of arthropods most commonly found fossilized.

SMALL IS BEAUTIFUL
Most trilobites were 1 to 4 in (3 to 10 cm) long. These are examples of *Elrathia*.

PRIZE POSSESSION
Trilobites are prized fossils. This Silurian *Calymene* has been made into a brooch. Examples of this species were found in such great numbers at Dudley, England, that they were nicknamed Dudley bugs.

Eyes

No eyes

TO SEE OR NOT TO SEE?
There were more than 10,000 different species of trilobites and all of them lived in the sea. Some crawled along the sea bed, others floated or swam through the water. Most species had two eyes and could probably see very well. Lenses are sometimes preserved in fossil trilobites because they were made of the mineral calcite. Some species, however, were eyeless. Most of these lived in darkness in the deep sea, beyond the depth to which natural light penetrates.

Trilobite *Dalmanites*

Trilobite *Concoryphe*

Modern millipede

Fossil millipede

EARLY SETTLERS
Like all arthropods, millipedes have bodies divided into segments, or sections. Unlike the other arthropods on these pages, they live on land and were among the first animals to do so. Fossil millipedes are seldom found.

Packed lenses

MULTIVISION
Trilobite eyes are the most ancient visual systems known. They consisted of many separate lenses packed together. Each lens produced its own image.

Echinocaris, a Devonian shrimplike arthropod

ROLL UP!
Some trilobites were able to roll up like wood lice, probably for protection against predators.

TRI-LOBED
The name trilobite was given to these creatures because their exoskeletons are divided into three distinct lobes, or parts. The soft parts and the legs on the lower surface of the animal were very seldom preserved. Whole fossil trilobites are surprisingly rare, but they can be found in rocks from the Cambrian to the Permian Period (about 590 to 250 million years old). They became extinct after that. This one is *Paradoxides* from the Cambrian. One of the biggest of all trilobites, it grew to 1 ft 7 in (50 cm) long.

Long spine

PRICKLY CUSTOMER
This Devonian trilobite, *Dicranurus*, was notable for its long spines, which are superbly preserved in this specimen.

Lobster's claw

Folded claws

LOBSTER CONCRETION
Lobsters belong to a group of arthropods called crustaceans. Although they have hard shells, crustaceans are not often fossilized because the shells break down easily after death. This Eocene lobster, *Homarus*, has been preserved in a concretion (pp. 8–9).

Small crab attached to large crab

CHINA CRAB
This Cenozoic fossil crab from China looks very similar to its modern relative (left) except that it does not have the red coloration. The claws are folded inward and the ends of the legs have been broken off. If you look closely, you can see the shell of a smaller crab stuck to the right legs of the large crab.

Pincerlike claw for feeding and fighting

Lobster's body

HANDS UP!
A modern crab looking very aggressive with its pincerlike claws raised in the air. Crabs can use these claws for feeding as well as fighting.

Modern lobster

Fossil sea scorpion

ARMOR-PLATED
Barnacles are a type of crustacean. They are protected in a "shell" of hard plates. The barnacles wave their legs in the water to create a current which wafts small particles of food toward their mouths. The plated shells of barnacles are often found as fossils, especially in Cenozoic rocks. They are sometimes found clustered together and cemented firmly to hard surfaces such as boulders or the fossil shells of mollusks (pp. 18–21). This group of fossil barnacles come from the Pliocene period.

Modern barnacle

Plated shells

Fossil barnacles

Sea scorpion

TERROR OF THE SEA
Eurypterids, commonly known as sea scorpions, were ferocious hunters in the sea and in freshwater during the Paleozoic Era. They are related to true scorpions of today, and some even had stinging tails, but they could grow to over 6 ft 6 in (2 m) long!

Arms and spines

ECHINODERMS are a very distinctive group of animals which all live in the sea. Among them are sea urchins (echinoids), sea lilies (crinoids), starfish (asteroids), and brittlestars (ophiuroids). The distinguishing feature of most echinoderms is their fivefold radial symmetry. That is, their bodies can be divided into five similar segments, kind of like the segments of an orange. As echinoderms have skeletons made of calcite, they are often found fossilized. Indeed, fossil echinoderms range back to the Cambrian. Echinoderm skeletons consist of many individual pieces or plates, each grown as a single crystal of calcite. These are often separated and scattered soon after the animal dies, so rapid burial is especially important to ensure good preservation.

Modern brittlestar

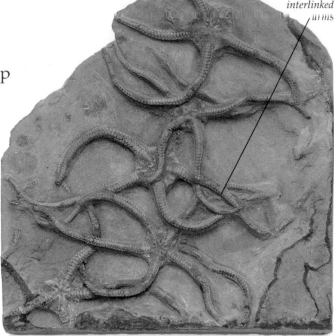

Delicate interlinked arms

BURIED ALIVE
This exceptional Jurassic specimen shows a group of five fossil brittlestars with arms interlinked. These may have been buried while still alive, as the plated skeletons are normally scattered soon after death. Brittlestars look like starfish but are more delicate and their arms break off easily, hence their name. They use their arms to move across the sea bed. Some feed on plankton; others are scavengers.

Symmetrical arm

Modern *Protoreaster*

STAR HUNTER
Many starfish are very efficient hunters, often feeding on clams and oysters which they open using the suckers on their arms. Others, like this Australian *Protoreaster*, extract their food from sediments such as sand.

STAR OF THE BEACH
Starfish are familiar to anyone who has explored tide pools and beaches by the sea, but they are very seldom found as fossils.

Mouth

Suckers

Underside of modern starfish

Position of missing arm

Mouth

Ammonite

ARM ROBBERY
This fossil starfish from the Jurassic, seen from underneath, is remarkably similar to some present-day species but unfortunately one of its arms is missing. Its mouth can be seen in the center. The rock in which it is embedded contains small ammonites and many shell fragments as well.

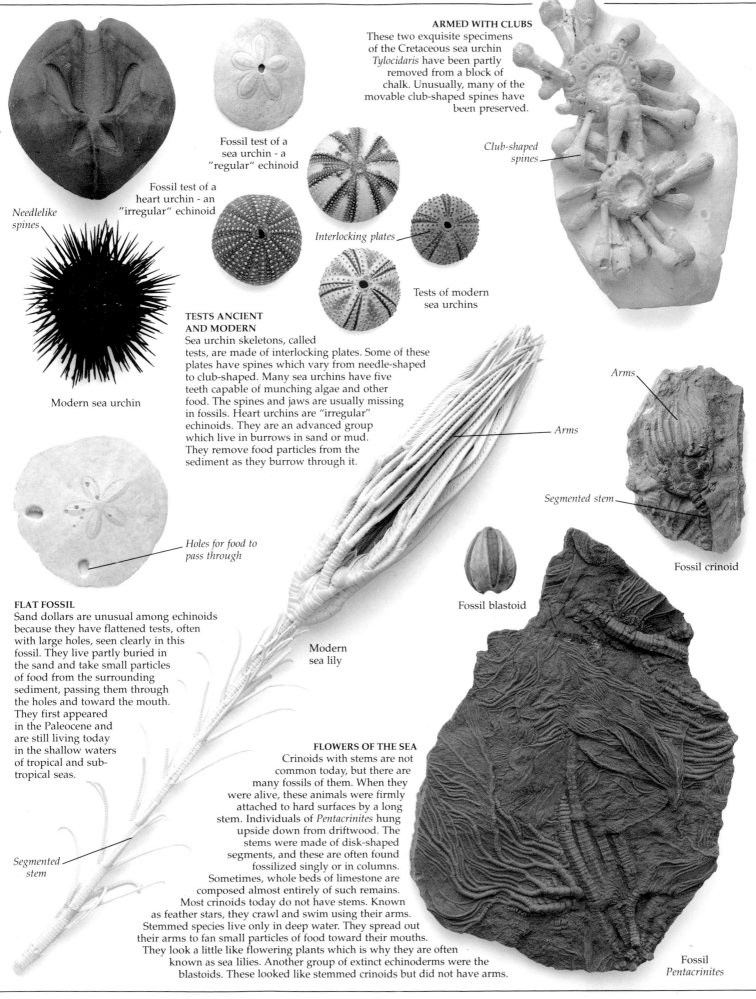

ARMED WITH CLUBS
These two exquisite specimens of the Cretaceous sea urchin *Tylocidaris* have been partly removed from a block of chalk. Unusually, many of the movable club-shaped spines have been preserved.

Club-shaped spines

Fossil test of a sea urchin - a "regular" echinoid

Fossil test of a heart urchin - an "irregular" echinoid

Interlocking plates

Tests of modern sea urchins

Needlelike spines

Modern sea urchin

TESTS ANCIENT AND MODERN
Sea urchin skeletons, called tests, are made of interlocking plates. Some of these plates have spines which vary from needle-shaped to club-shaped. Many sea urchins have five teeth capable of munching algae and other food. The spines and jaws are usually missing in fossils. Heart urchins are "irregular" echinoids. They are an advanced group which live in burrows in sand or mud. They remove food particles from the sediment as they burrow through it.

Arms

Arms

Segmented stem

Fossil crinoid

Fossil blastoid

Holes for food to pass through

FLAT FOSSIL
Sand dollars are unusual among echinoids because they have flattened tests, often with large holes, seen clearly in this fossil. They live partly buried in the sand and take small particles of food from the surrounding sediment, passing them through the holes and toward the mouth. They first appeared in the Paleocene and are still living today in the shallow waters of tropical and sub-tropical seas.

Modern sea lily

Segmented stem

FLOWERS OF THE SEA
Crinoids with stems are not common today, but there are many fossils of them. When they were alive, these animals were firmly attached to hard surfaces by a long stem. Individuals of *Pentacrinites* hung upside down from driftwood. The stems were made of disk-shaped segments, and these are often found fossilized singly or in columns. Sometimes, whole beds of limestone are composed almost entirely of such remains. Most crinoids today do not have stems. Known as feather stars, they crawl and swim using their arms. Stemmed species live only in deep water. They spread out their arms to fan small particles of food toward their mouths. They look a little like flowering plants which is why they are often known as sea lilies. Another group of extinct echinoderms were the blastoids. These looked like stemmed crinoids but did not have arms.

Fossil *Pentacrinites*

Fishes

FISHES are the most primitive vertebrates (animals with backbones). They are a very varied group, with about 20,000 species, and they use gills to breathe and fins to swim. Some fishes live in the sea and some in fresh water; others migrate between these environments. Fishes first appeared about 500 million years ago. Most were small, jawless, and covered with heavy armor. In the Devonian period, often referred to as the Age of Fishes, fishes became numerous, and early representatives of the major living groups were present. Skeletons of fossil fishes can be abundant in certain areas, but it is more common to find isolated teeth, especially of sharks.

Sparnodus part

FIN SPINE
Sharks and rays have skeletons made of cartilage, which is softer than bone and not usually fossilized. However, fossils of their teeth and spines stretch back to the Devonian. This is the spine of a Jurassic shark. It supported a large fin on the shark's back.

Dorsal fin

Impression of a modern shark

Sharp teeth

Teeth of an Eocene sand shark, *Eugomphodus*

ARMORED FISHES
One of the first known fishes with jaws was a group of armored fishes called placoderms. Some used their two arms to prop themselves up on the beds of rivers and freshwater lakes.

TOOTH FOR A TOOTH
Most sharks are fierce predators with a mass of sharp teeth arranged in whorls. New teeth are growing all the time to replace older teeth that drop out. The largest modern shark on record, a great white, was 29 ft 6 in (9 m) long. This is small in comparison with its extinct relative, *Carcharodon*, whose tooth (right) is 4 in (11 cm) long, suggesting a body length of over 39 ft (12 m).

Tooth of Pliocene shark, *Carcharodon*

Modern ray

JAWLESS FISHES
Cephalaspids were primitive freshwater fishes. They were jawless, and fed by sucking sediment from lakes or riverbeds.

Ptychodus tooth

Ridges for crushing food

SHELL CRUSHERS
Fossil teeth like these are all that is known of the cartilaginous fish *Ptychodus*, which was probably similar to a modern ray. It had ridged teeth, which it used to crush the shells of the mollusks on which it fed.

Ridged Ptychodus tooth

Well-preserved skeleton

FISH EATS FISH *right*
Fossils seldom provide direct evidence of an animal's diet. However, this remarkable Cretaceous dogfish contains the head of a teleost that it swallowed. The dogfish had very small teeth and would probably not have been able to bite the head off the body of a live fish. It seems more likely that the dogfish scavenged the head from a dead fish.

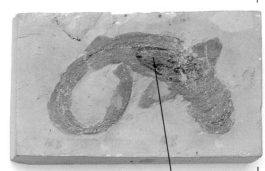

Swallowed fish head

Sparnodus counterpart

TWO PARTS
This slab of Eocene limestone has split through a fine fossil specimen of *Sparnodus*. The two pieces are called the part (left) and the counterpart (above). Bones of the skeleton, including the fins, are preserved in remarkable detail. *Sparnodus* belongs to a group of bony fishes still living today, known as porgies or sea breams.

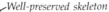

Thick scales covering the body

THICK-SCALED FISH
Lepidotes was a Mesozoic (pp. 12–13) bony fish. It was common all over the world, and some examples grew to a length of 6 ft 6 in (2 m). The body was covered by thick scales, and the button-shaped teeth, called toadstones in folklore, were probably used to crush mollusk shells.

Sharp predator's teeth

EAR STONES
Otoliths, or ear stones, are balance organs from the ears of fishes. They are made of chalky material and form unusual fossils. These examples are from Eocene fishes.

Modern African lungfish

Thick scales

TEETH FOR HUNTING
Related to the modern bowfin, *Caturus* is from the Jurassic. By the look of its sharp teeth it was a predator.

Armored head

BONY FISHES
About 200 million years ago, this primitive teleost, a type of bony fish, lived in the seas. It had small teeth, which suggests that it fed on tiny plankton, possibly living in schools like today's herring. Teleosts first appeared in the Triassic, and today they are the most common fishes. They include carp, salmon, cod, mackerel, flounder, and many others.

Remains of concretion

EXPOSED WITH ACID
Unlike modern lungfishes, which live in fresh water, the Devonian lungfish *Chirodipterus* lived in shallow seas. It had thick, bony scales and an armored head. This specimen from Australia was preserved in a hard, chalky concretion (pp. 8–9). It has been exposed by treatment in acid, which dissolved the concretion but not the fish within.

Plants-the pioneers

JET JEWELRY
Jet is a special kind of fossil wood which is dense enough to be carved and polished for jewelry. The formation of jet probably occurred when wood from monkey puzzle trees (opposite) was washed into the sea by rivers.

Impression in sandstone of the bark of *Lepidodendron*

THE INVASION OF THE LAND BY PLANTS about 410 million years ago was a key event in the history of life. It paved the way for colonization by animals and was the starting point for the development of the variety of plants we see today. Plants growing on the land had to be strong enough to support themselves against gravity, resistant to drying, and able to transport water, gathered by the roots, up to the higher portions of the plant where energy-producing photosynthesis occurred. These adaptations were first seen among the primitive land plants such as club mosses, horsetails, and ferns of the late Paleozoic. Examples from all of these groups are living today, though often in greatly reduced numbers. The flowering plants which dominate modern floras did not appear until the Cretaceous.

JOHANN SCHEUCHZER
The Swiss naturalist and physician Johann Scheuchzer (1672–1733) studied fossil plants and fishes from the Miocene rocks at Oeningen in Switzerland.

Diamond-shaped leaf scars

Lepidodendron

Cross-section of the fossil cone *Lepidostrobus*

Fossil *Baragwanathia*

Carboniferous club moss *Archaeosigillaria*

Club mosses

Club mosses, which belong to a group of plants called lycopods, reproduce by spores which are held in cones. Lycopods were common during the Paleozoic; *Baragwanathia* from the Devonian of Australia is probably the oldest known example. Some modern club mosses have creeping stems, unlike the Paleozoic lycopods which grew as trees. *Lepidodendron* reached 130 ft (40 m) tall. The fossil bark of *Lepidodendron* has a diamond pattern on it made by scars left when the leaves fell off. The fossil cones of *Lepidodendron* have been named *Lepidostrobus*.

Modern club moss *Lycopodium*

Archaeopteris, an extinct tree which reproduced by spores and grew up to 98 ft (30 m) tall

Modern asparagus "fern"
Asparagus setaceus

Toward the seed

The oldest ferns are of Devonian age. Club mosses declined after the Paleozoic, but ferns did not. They are common fossils in Mesozoic rocks and about 10,000 species are alive today. They have spore cases on the underside of their leaves. Tree ferns such as *Psaronius* grew alongside club moss trees in the coal forests of the Carboniferous (pp. 32–33). Most modern tree ferns are not closely related to these Paleozoic forms but belong to two families which appear in the Jurassic. The leaves of the now-extinct seed ferns often resemble true fern leaves but they were, in fact, relatives of more advanced, seed-bearing plants (pp. 30–31).

COMPRESSED FERN
Carbonized (turned to coal) leaves of the Jurassic fern *Coniopteris* are here preserved as compressions.

Plants in a typical Paleozoic scene

FAMILIAR FERN
Iodites from the Jurassic is a typical fern – the fronds are very similar to many modern species.

POLISHED FERN
This sectioned and polished piece of fossil wood is from the tree fern *Psaronius,* which grew to a height of 26 ft (8 m).

FOSSIL MONKEY PUZZLE CONES
One cone has been sectioned to show the internal structure.

WIDESPREAD SEED FERN
The presence of fossils of this seed fern, *Glossopteris*, in India, Africa, South America, Australia, and Antarctica provides evidence that these areas were once linked together as Gondwanaland (pp. 6–7).

Leathery leaf

Modern monkey puzzle branch

MONKEY PUZZLE
The monkey puzzle is a primitive type of conifer (pp. 30–31) first appearing in the Triassic. Today they live in the Andes mountains in South America. The tightly packed leathery leaves may live for 15 years before falling off the branch.

HORSETAILS
Horsetails date from the Devonian. Some grew as trees in the coal forests (pp. 32–33), reaching heights of 60 ft (18 m). This is the stem of a Jurassic *Equisetites*.

The only modern horsetail genus, *Equisetum*, which grows to about 5 ft (1.5 m) tall

Leaf-bearing part of stem

Equisetites

Underground part of stem

Continued on next page

Protected seeds

Most modern seed-producing plants have their seeds protected in a fruit (flowering plants, called angiosperms) or a cone (gymnosperms, including conifers). Angiosperms are the most successful of modern plants. There are an estimated 250,000 species, as compared with 50,000 species of all other plants. Grasses, oaks, tulips, palms, potatoes, and cacti are angiosperms. In spite of their great variety, angiosperms appear relatively late in the fossil record. The earliest examples come from the Cretaceous. The earliest conifer fossils occur earlier, in the Carboniferous.

SOFT FRUIT
All fruits contain seeds of some sort. Soft fruits decay quickly. Hard seeds are more likely to be fossilized.

Palm-like leaf

BEFORE THE FLOWERS
When angiosperms first appeared, some of the most common plants were cycads – palmlike gymnosperms which produced seeds in separate conelike structures. Modern cycads still look like palms. There are nine kinds living in tropical and subtropical forests.

Fossil cycad

Annual rings preserved in stone

CYCAD COMPANION
Other gymnosperms were also living at this time, and some Cretaceous conifer wood has been petrified (turned to stone). Petrification has preserved remarkable details of the original wood.

Petrified conifer wood

Sabal *leaf*

FOSSIL PALM
There are two main types of angiosperms - monocotyledons and dicotyledons. Monocotyledons generally have leaves with parallel veins; dicotyledons usually have net-veined leaves. Palms, like this *Sabal* from the Eocene, are monocotyledons, as are grasses. All other angiosperms shown are dicotyledons.

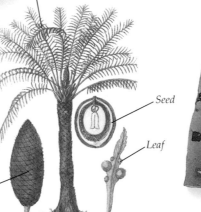
Palm-like tree
Seed
Leaf
"Cone"
Modern cycad

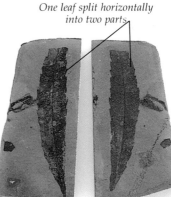
One leaf split horizontally into two parts

SPLIT IN TWO
Angiosperm leaves are relatively common and well preserved in some fine-grained sedimentary rocks. This Miocene example of a myrtle leaf has been fractured into two parts.

Leaf of a modern palm

Fossil *Nipa* fruit

COAST GUARDS
A fruit of a modern *Nipa* tree is compared here with a smaller fossil *Nipa* fruit from the Eocene. *Nipa* is a stemless palm which grows today along tropical coastlines or rivers close to the coast. It plays an important role in preventing coastal erosion.

Modern *Nipa* fruit

FLAT CHESTNUT
This is the flattened seed of a water chestnut from the Miocene.

Fossil poplar leaf

SMALL CHANGE
Fossil poplar leaves are almost identical to present-day poplar leaves. This beautiful example is about 25 million years old. Modern poplar trees can grow to 130 ft (40 m) tall; during its lifetime, each tree sheds a huge number of leaves that could become fossils.

Modern poplar leaves

Juglans seeds

Palliopora seeds

Mastixia seeds

Tectocarya seeds

Greatly magnified fossil pollen

ANCIENT SEEDS
Angiosperm seeds are often enclosed in a fleshy fruit eaten by animals, which then scatter the seeds. Various types of fossil fruits and seeds are common from the late Cretaceous onward. All those shown here are about 30 million years old.

FIRST POLLEN
This Cretaceous pollen grain is one of the earliest-known types of angiosperm pollen.

GIANT CONIFER
Giant redwoods are conifers now only living in North America. Remains can be found in Jurassic and younger rocks. Conifers are gymnosperms; that is, they produce seeds inside cones. Fossils include rooted stumps and fallen trunks as well as cones and seeds.

Fossil Miocene leaves

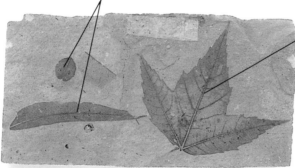

Fossil maple leaf showing midrib and veins

LEAVES IMPRESSIONS
These Miocene leaves are beautifully preserved as impressions in a fine-grained limestone. The three-lobed leaf with midrib and delicate veins is easy to identify as that of a maple, even though very little of the original plant tissue remains.

Leaves of a modern maple

Bud

STONE RINGS
Growth rings, like those that can be seen in the wood of trees living today, show clearly in this polished section of petrified oak wood. They provide useful information about the seasonal growth of the tree, and the climate at the time the tree was living.

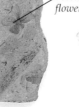

BUDDING MAPLE
Buds are rarely preserved in fossil plants but, remarkably, one is attached to this flattened twig of a Miocene maple tree.

Fossil flower

PRESERVED PETALS
Although fossils of flowering plants are common, the flowers themselves are seldom found, since they are delicate and short-lived. Therefore, these petals of *Porana* from the Miocene are exceptional. A flower of today with similar petals is the primrose.

Modern primrose

Growth rings

Fossil fuels

Oil and coal are known as fossil fuels because they originate from ancient organisms, mainly plants. When we burn them we release the energy, in the form of heat and light, which was originally captured by the living plants during photosynthesis millions of years ago. Fossil fuels are extracted from the Earth in huge quantities. In addition to being a source of energy, they are also used in the manufacture of many synthetic materials.

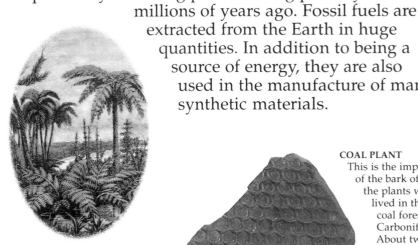

A coal forest

MODERN MINING
Most coal is extracted by deep mining. When the coal is near the surface, it is extracted by strip mining.

COAL LABOR
Wagons full of coal were once hauled through the underground tunnels by men, women, and children. Nowadays, there are conveyor belts, or trucks pulled by engines.

COAL PLANT
This is the impression of the bark of one of the plants which lived in the vast coal forests of the Carboniferous. About two-thirds of the world's coal supplies were formed by the plants of these forests.

From plant to coal

Coal is formed after millions of years by the decay and burial of plants that usually grow in freshwater swamps. Special conditions are needed for coal to form. During the early stages of the process, oxygen must not be present so that bacterial decay of the plants can lead to the formation of peat. The peat is then buried and compressed under the weight of more sediment and rotting plants. It undergoes chemical changes resulting first in lignite, then bituminous coal, and finally, if temperatures and pressures become sufficiently high, anthracite coal.

Living mosses and grasses

PEAT
The plants growing on top of this peat will eventually die and add their rotting remains to the peat beneath. Dried peat is sometimes used as a household fuel.

Crack caused when drying

LIGNITE
Lignite, the first stage of coal formation, is typically dark brown and may still contain some water. Lignite crumbles easily and may crack as it dries in the air.

Impression of lycopod bark

BITUMINOUS COAL
Black bituminous coal is sometimes used as a fuel for household heating. The impression of a Carboniferous lycopod tree (pp. 28–29) seen here shows the plant origin of the coal.

Ink

Shoe polish

ALL MADE FROM COAL
Most coal is burned to provide heat or to make steam which, in turn, is used to drive the generators in power stations producing electricity. But many everyday products used in the home and garden are also made from coal. These include coal-tar soap, ink, and shoe polish. Other products sometimes made from coal are antiseptics, drugs, dyes, detergents, perfumes, nail polish, fertilizers, weed-killers, insecticides, nylon, and plastics.

Coal-tar soap

ANTHRACITE
Anthracite is a hard, intensely black and shiny coal. It is the best-quality coal.

OIL PLANT

This is a greatly enlarged fossil of a microscopic Eocene plant which lived in the sea. Similar planktonic plants were the originators of oil. Their fossilized remains provide important clues about rocks, useful to geologists searching for oil.

NO OIL

This core of rock, cut during drilling for geologists to examine, does not contain any oil.

OIL-BEARING

This dark piece of porous core does contain oil. Oil does not form huge underground lakes but is held as tiny droplets in the pores in the rock – as water is held in a sponge.

From plankton to oil

Oil and natural gas are together known as petroleum, from the Latin words *petra* (rock) and *oleum* (oil). They were formed mainly by the decomposition of tiny planktonic plants which lived near the surface of the sea. When they died, their remains sank to the sea bed and were buried in mud. Over millions of years, this mud turned to rock, and the organic remains formed specks of carbon-rich kerogen, an early stage of oil, and then oil. Oil is often found some distance away from where it originated. It migrates, or moves, generally upward through porous rocks which have tiny spaces into which it can seep. If it meets an impervious layer of rock – that is, rock which has no pores – the oil cannot migrate. It may therefore become trapped in what is then called a "reservoir rock."

Modern oil rig

Three cones of the bit

DRILLING FOR OIL

The most common drill bit is a tri-cone bit like this one. Bits cut through rock by being rotated at the bottom of a hollow drill pipe down which a muddy fluid is pumped. This fluid lubricates and cools the bit and carries away the fragments of rock.

Heavy crude oil

An early way of drilling for oil

Fossil foraminifers

MICROSCOPIC FOSSILS

Fossils of foraminifers – microscopic animals with chalky shells – are often used by geologists to date rocks.

Polyester scarf

Sunglasses

CRUDE OILS

It can be extremely difficult to get oil out of rock. Often, the presence of natural gas helps force the oil up to the surface, but sometimes pressure is too low and the oil has to be pumped up. Crude oils – oils in their natural state – vary widely. The heaviest oils, formed at relatively low temperatures, are black, thick, and waxy. The lightest oils, formed at high temperatures, are pale and thin. All crude oils must be refined before they can be used.

Light crude oil

Crayons

REFINED OIL

Oils are treated in a refinery. Refining is a very complex process involving several different stages.

ALL MADE FROM OIL

Once in the refinery, oil is separated into different liquids, gases, and solids. These are used to make a wide range of products in addition to gasoline, diesel fuel, and lubricating oil. Many detergents, paints, plastics, and clothes are derived from petroleum chemicals. These crayons, sunglasses, and polyester scarf are all byproducts of oil.

Out of the water

CURIOUS CREATURE
This curious amphibian, *Diplocaulus*, from the Permian of Texas, lived in ponds and streams.

COLONIZATION OF THE LAND by vertebrates 350 million years ago was made possible through the evolution of lungs for breathing air, and limbs for walking. Air-breathing was inherited by the first land vertebrates, amphibians, from their fish ancestors. Fishes with lungs for breathing – lungfishes (pp.26–27) – still exist today. The Australian lungfish can gulp fresh air from the surface of drying ponds while other fishes die in the foul water. Limbs for walking developed from muscular fins similar to those seen in the living coelacanth. Most amphibians have a larval stage (tadpole) which has to live in water, and for this reason amphibians must return to water to lay their eggs.

Fleshy outline of the body

Long hind legs

FOSSIL FROG
This fossil frog is a female of a species of *Discoglossus*. It comes from the Miocene of West Germany. The specimen is unusual in showing the fleshy outline of the body and long hind legs. Frogs first appeared in the Triassic but are seldom found fossilized because their delicate bones decay very easily.

Eyes

FOSSIL TADPOLE
Even rarer than fossils of adult frogs are fossils of their tadpoles. The two eyes can be clearly seen in this Cenozoic specimen of *Pelobates*.

ETERNAL YOUTH
The axolotl is an unusual salamander from Central America. It remains in a "larval" stage throughout its life, using its feathery external gills to breathe underwater and not coming onto land. The name axolotl comes from an appropriate Aztec word meaning "water doll."

GOING THROUGH STAGES
Like most amphibians, frogs usually have to lay their eggs in water. The eggs hatch into tadpoles which live in the water. As they develop, tadpoles go through different stages before they leave the water as miniature frogs. Lungs replace gills as a means of breathing, front and back legs grow, and the tail gradually disappears.

Heavy hip bones

SURVIVING AMPHIBIAN
The early inhabitants of the land differed in many ways from the amphibians which have survived to the present day such as frogs, toads, newts, and salamanders. This is a modern natterjack toad.

Strong foot

EARLY ANCESTOR
One of the earliest known amphibians, *Ichthyostega*, is found in Devonian rocks in Greenland. It is regarded by some paleontologists as an ancestor of all later amphibians. It was apparently able to walk on land and had lungs for breathing air, but still had a tail fin like a fish.

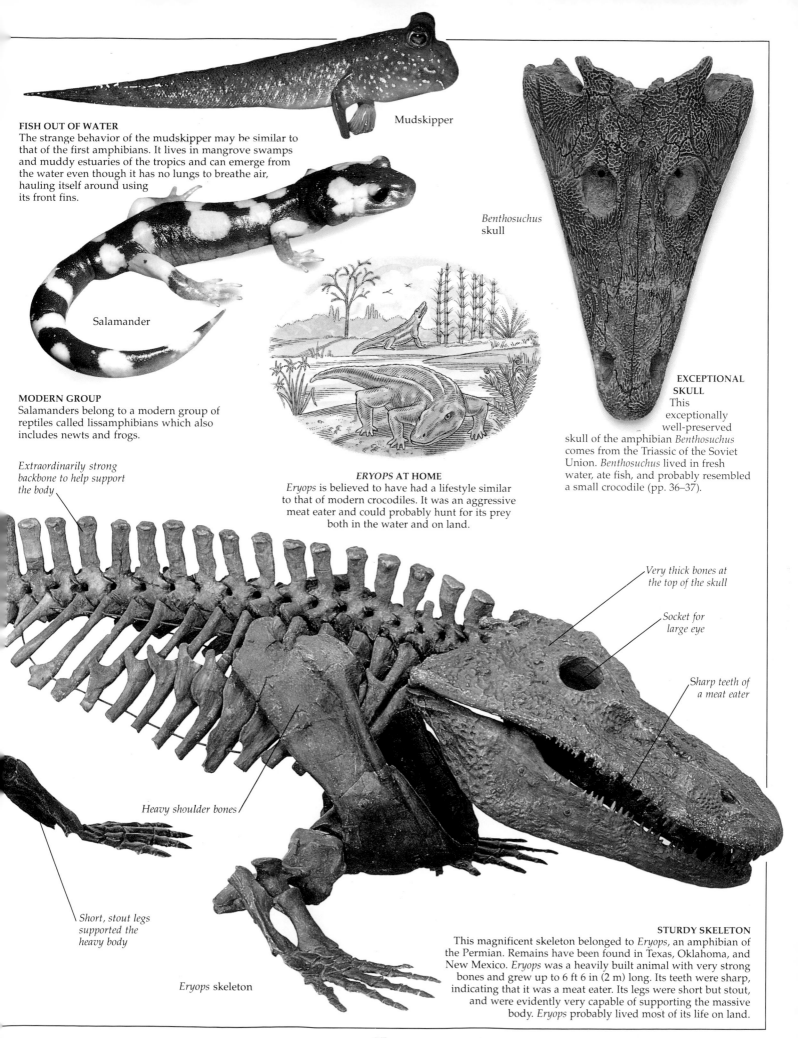

Mudskipper

FISH OUT OF WATER
The strange behavior of the mudskipper may be similar to that of the first amphibians. It lives in mangrove swamps and muddy estuaries of the tropics and can emerge from the water even though it has no lungs to breathe air, hauling itself around using its front fins.

Salamander

MODERN GROUP
Salamanders belong to a modern group of reptiles called lissamphibians which also includes newts and frogs.

Benthosuchus skull

EXCEPTIONAL SKULL
This exceptionally well-preserved skull of the amphibian *Benthosuchus* comes from the Triassic of the Soviet Union. *Benthosuchus* lived in fresh water, ate fish, and probably resembled a small crocodile (pp. 36–37).

Extraordinarily strong backbone to help support the body

***ERYOPS* AT HOME**
Eryops is believed to have had a lifestyle similar to that of modern crocodiles. It was an aggressive meat eater and could probably hunt for its prey both in the water and on land.

Very thick bones at the top of the skull

Socket for large eye

Sharp teeth of a meat eater

Heavy shoulder bones

Short, stout legs supported the heavy body

Eryops skeleton

STURDY SKELETON
This magnificent skeleton belonged to *Eryops*, an amphibian of the Permian. Remains have been found in Texas, Oklahoma, and New Mexico. *Eryops* was a heavily built animal with very strong bones and grew up to 6 ft 6 in (2 m) long. Its teeth were sharp, indicating that it was a meat eater. Its legs were short but stout, and were evidently very capable of supporting the massive body. *Eryops* probably lived most of its life on land.

Onto the land

THREE MAIN KINDS OF REPTILES live today: lizards and snakes, tortoises and turtles, and crocodiles. A fourth is represented only by the tuatara. The number of surviving reptiles is much less than the number of extinct forms, especially those which lived in Mesozoic times such as dinosaurs (pp. 40–43), pterosaurs, and ichthyosaurs and plesiosaurs (pp. 38–39). The first reptile fossils are found in rocks from the early Carboniferous, about 300 million years old. It is thought that these early reptiles possessed two important features, still seen in modern species, that enabled them to live away from water unlike amphibians: a special kind of egg, known as an amniote egg (below), and a scaly skin which protected their bodies against drying out.

There are over 2,000 species of snakes living today

BODY GUARD
Trionyx is a turtle from the Eocene. Only the protective carapace, or shell, is preserved here – the bones are missing. The first turtles appeared in the Triassic and probably lacked the ability of modern species to withdraw their head, limbs, and tail completely. Another difference is that they had teeth, which are replaced in modern species by a sharp, horny beak for slicing vegetation or meat.

READY FOR LAND
Turtle eggs contain liquid and are protected by leathery shells. Before birth an embryo can develop through early stages into an animal able to breathe and live on land.

BURIED EGGS
Sea-going turtles return to land to lay their eggs, which they bury in the warm sands of tropical beaches, and then return to the sea. The largest living turtle is the leatherback, which may reach 8 ft (2.5 m) in length. The Cretaceous turtle *Archelon* grew to more than 13 ft (4 m) long!

Modern ladder snake

LEGLESS VERTEBRATE
The earliest fossil snakes come from the late Cretaceous. Snakes have a poor fossil record but vertebrae are occasionally found. These vertebrae of *Paleophis*, from the Paleocene of Mali, West Africa, were found separately but have been assembled to give an impression of one snake's backbone. Snakes probably evolved from a lizard-like ancestor, with their limbs getting smaller and smaller and eventually disappearing altogether. This is thought to have been the result of the animal adopting a burrowing lifestyle, which was later abandoned by true snakes. Two important features seen in modern snakes are the poisonous fangs, used to inject venom into prey, and the loosely connected skull bones, which enable the snake to open its mouth very wide to swallow large prey.

Sprawler

Semi-improved

Fully improved

GRADUAL IMPROVEMENT
The limb positions of reptiles gradually improved to support the weight of the body more efficiently. The different postures can still be seen today. Lizards are "sprawlers"; crocodiles have a "semi-improved" posture and are able to lift their bellies off the ground to move in a hurry. "Fully improved" animals include all the dinosaurs and also advanced mammals.

Long body

Scaly skin prevents drying out

Flattened skull

Powerful jaws

BABY PREDATOR
Crocodiles have changed little in appearance since the Jurassic – they all have long bodies, short legs, a flattened skull, and sharp teeth. Crocodiles (including alligators and gavials) are predators which swim slowly toward their prey before making a rapid grab with their powerful jaws.

Diplocynodon skull

CROCODILE HEAD
The largest fossil crocodile, *Deinosuchus,* from the Cretaceous of Texas, is estimated to have been 40–50 ft (12–15 m) long! This head belonged to an Oligocene crocodile, *Diplocynodon.*

Diagrams of a modern lizard

LONG LIZARD *right*
Because lizards generally live in dry, upland areas where the likelihood of burial is low, fossil examples are seldom found. The earliest examples are from the Triassic, and they were probably present in great numbers during the reign of their larger relatives the dinosaurs. This fossil lizard, *Adriosaurus,* had a very long body and is almost snakelike. Others had skin stretched between extended ribs so they were evidently able to glide through the air, like the modern "flying dragon" *Draco volans,* found in the East Indies.

Sea dragons

During Mesozoic times, when dinosaurs roamed the land, the seas were inhabited by several kinds of giant reptiles popularly known as sea dragons. The most numerous of these were the ichthyosaurs and plesiosaurs; a third group, the mosasaurs, became common toward the end of the Mesozoic. None of these marine reptiles was really a dragon, of course, but their remains may have contributed to the legends of the long-necked, fire-breathing monsters. Their ways of life were similar to modern marine mammals such as small whales, dolphins, and seals. Some were fish eaters; others ate belemnites (pp. 20–21) and other mollusks (pp. 18–21). They all breathed air and were therefore forced to surface regularly. Ichthyosaurs, plesiosaurs, and mosasaurs all became extinct, as did the dinosaurs, about 65 million years ago at the end of the Cretaceous.

MARY ANNING
Mary Anning (1799–1847) is famous for the fossils she collected close to her home in Lyme Regis on the south coast of England. The cliffs here contain abundant fossils of animals which lived in the sea in Jurassic times. Between 1810 and 1812 Mary and her brother excavated a complete ichthyosaur (at the time thought to be a crocodile) which they sold for £23, a large sum of money in those days.

A GOOD LIKENESS
The similarity in shape between modern dolphins and ichthyosaurs suggests they had a similar lifestyle.

Dorsal fin for steering

Backbone

Kink in backbone

Powerful tail for swimming

Pointed tooth

A mosasaur

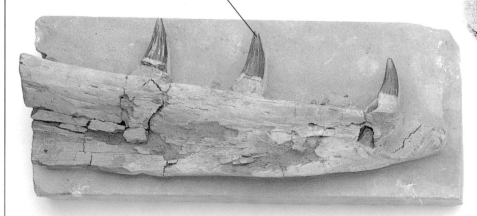

Excavation of a mosasaur jaw from a chalk mine at Maastricht in the Netherlands, in the 18th century.

JAW OF A GIANT LIZARD
Three pointed teeth are visible in this fragment of a mosasaur jaw from the Cretaceous. Mosasaurs were closely related to the land-dwelling monitor lizards of today. Mosasaurs grew up to 30 ft (9 m) long, and were probably slow-moving predators. They existed for a relatively short time in geological history, being known only from the late Cretaceous.

Ring of bones around eye socket

Short, sharp teeth

SAMUEL CLARKE
Samuel Clarke (1815–1898) was an amateur geologist who lived near Lyme Regis. He knew the area well and directed professionals to the most likely spots for finding sea dragons. He is holding the skull of a plesiosaur found in 1863.

PACKED TEETH
The long jaws of most ichthyosaurs are crammed with short, sharp teeth. Ichthyosaurs had large eyes, and it is thought that the ring of bones around the eye sockets improved their focusing ability. Their nostrils were far back on the top of the skull, as in modern dolphins and whales. This made it easier for the animals to breathe when they surfaced for air.

BATTLE OF THE SEA DRAGONS
A fictitious encounter between an ichthyosaur and a long-necked plesiosaur.

Outline of soft tissue

Neck vertebrae close together

Long jaws

Eye socket

Packed teeth

Paddle for steering

STREAMLINED PREDATOR
The streamlined shape of an ichthyosaur is seen in this fine Jurassic specimen in which an outline of the soft tissues has been preserved as well as the skeleton. The neck vertebrae of ichthyosaurs were close together so that the head ran smoothly into the body. This is typical of fast-swimming predators and is also seen in dolphins today. Ichthyosaurs swam by moving their powerful tails. Their backbones had a downward kink, as they extended only into the lower part of the tail fin. When the first skeletons were discovered, it was thought that these backbones were broken tails. The dorsal fin and paddles were used for steering and stability. Unlike most reptiles, ichthyosaurs gave birth to live young. Some specimens have been found with young inside the body cavity of adults, and several examples are known of mothers fossilized in the act of giving birth.

PADDLE POWER
The limbs of plesiosaurs formed large paddles. Like a turtle, a plesiosaur probably flapped these up and down when swimming.

TIME OF THE ICHTHYOSAURS
Dating back to the Triassic, ichthyosaurs were especially common in the Jurassic and survived into the late Cretaceous.

Fossil giants

THERE WERE MANY different species of dinosaurs, and their reign spanned 150 million years from the Triassic to the end of the Cretaceous. Dinosaurs were reptiles. Not all of them were huge; there were large ones and small ones. Some were plant eaters, others were meat eaters. Some had armored plates, others had spiked or clubbed tails. The variety was enormous. We know about dinosaurs from their skeletons, and detailed restorations of them can be made from their bones (pp. 10–11). We cannot know for certain what color they were but can make a guess based on the color of reptiles living today. The mystery of dinosaur extinction at the end of Cretaceous times has stimulated many different theories. Some scientists attribute the extinction to a change in the climate; others, to a change in the vegetation. Whatever the reason, the dinosaurs did not all die out at once. By the end of the Cretaceous, they were already reduced to fewer than twenty species.

FOOD GRINDER
Apatosaurus, a large Jurassic sauropod, weighed about 30 tons. Like all sauropods, it was a plant eater, probably using its long neck to reach leaves on trees. Its teeth were relatively small, and it is thought that *Apatosaurus* swallowed stones which then acted as a mill, grinding up the food in its stomach. Modern crocodiles use stones in a similar way.

MONSTER-STALKING
Although all the giant Mesozoic reptiles became extinct long before humans appeared, some people still search for living examples of these monsters.

Edmontosaurus

PLANT EATER
One of the last-surviving dinosaurs was *Edmontosaurus*. It was a hadrosaur, or duckbill, which grew to about 43 ft (13 m) long. Hadrosaurs were once thought to live partly in water, feeding on water plants, but land-plant fossils have been found with some skeletons, which suggests that a diet of trees and shrubs was more likely. These were dealt with by powerful teeth – about 1,000 in *Edmontosaurus*. Hadrosaurs laid their eggs in mound-shaped nests. A colony of closely grouped hadrosaur nests was discovered in Montana, indicating that the animals may have lived in herds. The nests had young of different ages in them so the adults apparently protected their young.

Skull of Edmontosaurus

Powerful teeth for crushing leaves

— Hypsilophodon *femur*

FLEET OF FOOT
This Cretaceous dinosaur, *Hypsilophodon*, grew up to about 6 ft 6 in (2 m) long. It was probably agile and swift, and has been compared with the modern gazelle.

— Apatosaurus *femur*

RARE EGG
Fragments of broken dinosaur eggs are fairly common, but complete eggs are rare. This *Protoceratops* egg was found in Mongolia in the 1920s and was part of the first evidence that dinosaurs laid eggs.

KING OF THE DINOSAURS
Perhaps the most famous of all dinosaurs, and one of the last, was *Tyrannosaurus*. This was the largest meat-eating animal ever to live on land. It was about 49 ft (15 m) long from head to tail. Its sharp, pointed teeth, seen in this skull, are a clear indication that it was a meat eater, possibly sometimes scavenging the carcasses of dead dinosaurs. Very few specimens of *Tyrannosaurus* have ever been found, and there is some doubt about the exact structure of the powerful tail and function of the tiny forelimbs.

Tyrannosaurus

KNEE BONES
There was a huge variation in size between different species of dinosaurs. One of the largest, *Brachiosaurus*, weighed about 54 tons – as much as 14 large elephants – while the smallest were the size of a chicken. To illustrate size variation, the femur (upper leg bone) of a *Hypsilophodon*, about 4 in (10 cm) long, is here placed on the equivalent bone of an *Apatosaurus*, about 6 ft 6 in (2 m) long.

Sharp, pointed teeth – up to 7 in (18 cm) long

Skull of *Tyrannosaurus*

Discovering dinosaurs

Iguanodon tooth

CLAWS DISCOVERER
Bill Walker holding the claw bone of *Baryonyx* which he discovered in 1983.

T**HE FIRST DESCRIPTIONS** of the fossil bones of dinosaurs were made over 150 years ago. First some teeth and then some bones of *Iguanodon* were found in southern England by the English doctor Gideon Mantell and his wife. Later, bones of the dinosaurs *Megalosaurus* and *Hylaeosaurus* were also discovered. In 1841, Sir Richard Owen, a leading British anatomist, invented the name dinosaur, which means "terrible lizard," for these early discoveries. They were followed by many more all around the world. Huge numbers of dinosaur remains were found in North America during the second half of the 19th century and into the 20th century, and other significant finds were made in Tanzania, China, and Mongolia. Important dinosaur discoveries are still being made of species already known and of new species. Almost every new discovery adds to our knowledge of these magnificent extinct reptiles.

MANTELL'S TOOTH!
This is one of the original *Iguanodon* teeth which were named by Mantell in 1825.

MANTELL'S QUARRY
Mantell was a doctor of medicine and an enthusiastic collector of fossils. The *Iguanodon* teeth and bones he described came from an old quarry in the Cuckfield area of southern England. Here rocks of early Cretaceous age were dug for use as gravel.

BIG REPTILE
In 1824, William Buckland discovered some dinosaur bones in Stonesfield in Oxfordshire, England. He gave the animal the name *Megalosaurus*, which means "big reptile." Buckland was a teacher of geology at the University of Oxford when he described his dinosaur. This jawbone belonged to a *Megalosaurus* and comes from the same area as Buckland's specimens.

BIG BUT NOT BIGGEST
Megalosaurus was a Jurassic meat eater related to the larger and better known *Tyrannosaurus* (p. 41).

EDWARD DRINKER COPE
Between 1870 and 1897 Cope took part in what has been described as the great dinosaur gold rush. It took place in the U.S., primarily in the states of Montana and Wyoming. Two names are especially associated with this gold rush - Cope and Marsh. Each hired independent teams of collectors to excavate dinosaur bones in the race to be first to describe the many new species.

OTHNIEL CHARLES MARSH
In this cartoon, Marsh is depicted as a circus ringmaster leading his team of prehistoric animals. The intense rivalry between Cope and Marsh caused the two men to swap a succession of insults, and even to destroy incomplete fossils in their own quarries in order to prevent future collection by their rival!

1 **EXTRACTING DINOSAUR BONES IN MONTANA.**
A drill is used to extract large bones. They are left surrounded by some rock, which is eventually removed in the laboratory.

2 **PROTECTING THE BONES**
The bones can be fragile. They are protected in a plaster jacket made by wrapping them in strips of scrim (open-weave fabric) soaked in a plaster of Paris paste. Sometimes the jacket is made of polyurethane foam.

3 **REMOVING THE BONES**
Once they have been carefully marked for future identification, the bones are removed from the cliff and transported to the laboratory for preparation. Large bones still embedded in rock can be heavy and awkward to handle. It may be easiest to maneuver them using a pulley.

CLAWS
An important dinosaur discovery of recent years was made by amateur collector Bill Walker. He unearthed a spectacular claw bone from a claypit in Surrey, England. Paleontologists at the Natural History Museum in London soon realized the importance of this find and excavated more bones. Popularly know as Claws, this dinosaur was a new species belonging to a new genus. It was named *Baryonyx walkeri* in honor of its discoverer.

Upper arm

Claw bone

Toe bone

FISH EATER
Baryonyx was unusual among dinosaurs because it fed on fish. Its head was shaped like that of a fish-eating crocodile, and fish scales were found in its rib cage.

What are rocks and minerals?

James Hutton (1726-97), one of the founders of modern geology

ROCKS ARE NATURAL AGGREGATES or combinations of one or more minerals. Some rocks, such as quartzite (pure quartz) and marble (pure calcite), contain only one mineral. Most, however, consist of more than one kind. Minerals are inorganic (nonliving) solids that are found in nature. They are made of elements such as silicon, oxygen, carbon, and iron. Here, two common rocks – granite and basalt – are shown with individual specimens of the major minerals of which they are formed. Rock-forming minerals can be divided into several groups – these are described in more detail on pages 66–67.

GRANITE AND ITS MAJOR MINERALS
Usually, several kinds of minerals are present in a rock, their size and texture varying according to how the rock formed. In granite, a coarse-grained, igneous rock, the three major minerals are visible to the naked eye. They are quartz (gray areas), feldspars (pink and white),and mica (black).

Quartz

Mica

Feldspar

Etched face

1 QUARTZ
Well-developed quartz crystals, like this group, may have milky, etched faces.

2 MICA
Black biotite (a type of mica) crystals can be split into wafer-thin sheets.

3 FELDSPAR
Crystals of orthoclase (a feldspar) may be milky white or pale pink.

BASALT AND ITS MAJOR MINERALS
Basalt consists mainly of three minerals - olivine, pyroxene, and plagioclase feld-spar. But because it is fine-grained, it is not always possible to tell them apart with the naked eye. This olivine basalt is from the crater of the Kilauea volcano in Hawaii.

1 OLIVINE
Transparent green crystals of olivine are quite rare, and are known as peridot (pp. 114–115).

2 FELDSPAR
Flat or polished crystals of labradorite, a plagioclase feldspar from Labrador, Canada, display a beautiful play of colors.

Iridescent blue and orange visible on the surface

Augite crystal

Rock matrix

3 PYROXENE
This well developed, single black crystal of augite (a pyroxene) comes from Italy. Augite crystals are found in various igneous rocks.

The scope of rock forms

Rocks and minerals occur in many different forms. Rocks do not necessarily have to be hard and resistant; loose sand and wet clay are considered to be rocks. The individual size of minerals in a rock ranges from millimeters, in a fine-grained volcanic rock, to several yards in a granite pegmatite.

ROCKS FORMED WITHIN ROCKS

This sedimentary rock specimen is a claystone septarian nodule. Nodules (knobs) such as this are formed when groundwater redistributes minerals within a rock in a particular pattern. Nodules are sometimes known as concretions. Here, the pattern of veins is formed of calcite.

ROCKS FORMED BY EVAPORATION

Stalactites are formed from substances that are deposited when dripping water evaporates (pp. 56–57). This spectacular pale blue stalactite is composed entirely of the mineral chalcanthite (copper sulfate) and formed from copper-rich waters in a mine.

Section of a mine roof colored with deposits of the copper mineral, chalcanthite

CRYSTALS FROM MINERAL ORE

Orange-red crystals of the mineral wulfenite from Arizona are formed in veins that carry lead and molybdenum.

Eruption of Mount Pelée, Martinique, on August 5, 1851

ROCKS FROM VOLCANIC ERUPTION

Despite its extraordinary appearance, "Pele's hair" is technically a rock. It consists of golden-brown hairlike fibers of basalt glass that sometimes enclose tiny olivine crystals, and was formed from the eruption of basaltic magma as a lava spray.

Lighter bands of pyroxene and plagioclase feldspar

Dark layer of chromite

ROCKS THAT FORM IN LAYERS

Norite is an igneous rock composed of the minerals pyroxene, plagioclase feldspar, and the chromium-rich mineral chromite. In this specimen from South Africa, the dark and light minerals have separated from each other so that the rock is layered. The dark chromite layers are an important source of chromium.

Weathering and erosion

ALL ROCKS BREAK DOWN at the Earth's surface. Weathering is mainly a chemical reaction, aided by the presence of water. Rocks are also broken down by mechanical processes involving rain, alternate freezing and thawing, the abrasive (scraping) action of sediment in water, wind and, ice.

Wind erosion

Constant attack by sediment in wind may slowly grind away at a rock and erode it.

MONUMENT VALLEY, ARIZONA
Large-scale abrasion by the wind produces huge, protruding landforms called buttes.

ABRASION BY THE WIND
The abrasive action of the wind wears away softer layers of rock and leaves the harder ones sticking out, as in this desert rock from East Africa.

SAND BLASTING
Faceted desert pebbles, formed by sand constantly being blown against them, are called dreikanters.

Weathering caused by temperature changes

Rock expands and contracts as the temperature changes, causing it to break up. Shattering is also caused when water in the rock freezes and expands.

Sandstone composed of sand collected 200 million years ago in a desert environment

Sand from a present-day desert in Saudi Arabia

DESERT EROSION
Rocks formed in desert conditions, where sediment is carried by wind, are often reddish in color and composed of characteristically rounded sand grains.

DESERT ENVIRONMENT
Wind and temperature changes cause continual weathering and bizarre, barren landscapes in the Sahara Desert.

ONION-SKIN WEATHERING
In this type of weathering, changes in temperature cause the surface layers of rock to expand, contract, and finally peel away from the underlying rock.

Fine-grained dolerite

Onion-skin weathered dolerite

Peeling layers like onion skins, caused by changes in temperature

Chemical weathering

Only a few minerals can resist weathering by rainwater, which is a weak acid. Minerals dissolved at the surface may be carried down and redeposited in the soil and rock below.

Fresh, unaltered granite

Coarse, weathered granite

GRANITE TORS
Tors, weathered rounded rocks, are formed of the remains left when the surrounding rocks have been eroded away. This example is on Dartmoor, England.

Gossan altered by groundwater

ALTERED MINERALS
Granite is split by the expansion of water as it freezes. Its minerals are then chemically altered, producing coarse rock fragments.

Secondary minerals

CHEMICAL CHANGES
Chemical weathering of an ore vein may cause redistribution of minerals. The bright-colored minerals were formed from deposits of minerals that dissolved from rocks at higher levels. They are called secondary deposits.

TROPICAL WEATHERING
In certain tropical climates, quartz is dissolved and carried away, while feldspars are altered to clay minerals that may collect on the surface as a thick deposit of bauxite (pp. 70–71).

Ice erosion

As glaciers move they pick up fragments of rock which become frozen into the base of the ice. The moving, frozen mass causes further erosion of underlying rocks.

Large rock fragment

Scratches caused by a glacier

PARTHENON, ATHENS, GREECE
Chemicals in the air can react with stone and cause drastic weathering. This can be seen on the Parthenon and on gargoyles on buildings.

SCRATCHED ROCK
The deep gouge marks on this limestone from Grindelwald, Switzerland, were caused by abrasive rock fragments contained in the glacier that flowed over it.

GLACIER DEPOSITS
A till is a deposit left by a melting glacier and contains crushed rock fragments ranging from microscopic grains to large pebbles. Ancient tills that have become packed into hard rock are called tillite. This specimen is from the Flinders Range in South Australia, which was covered with glaciers some 600 million years ago.

MORTERATSCH GLACIER, SWITZERLAND *left*
Glaciers are a major cause of erosion in mountainous regions.

Rocks on the seashore

AT THE SEASHORE, geological processes can be seen taking place. Many seashores are backed by cliffs, beneath which is a deposit of coarse material that has fallen from above. This is gradually broken up by the sea and sorted into pebbles, gravel, sand, and mud. Then the various sizes of sediment are deposited separately – this is the raw material for future sedimentary rocks (pp. 54–55).

Pebbles on Chesil Beach, England

GRADED GRAINS
On the beach, these pebbles are sorted by wave and tide action. The sand comes from a nearby area. It is pure quartz; the other rock-forming minerals were washed away by constant wave movement.

Large, coarse pebbles

Mica schist

Irregularly shaped pyrite nodule

SKIMMING STONES
As every schoolchild knows, the best stones for skimming are disk-shaped. They are most likely to be sedimentary or meta-morphic rocks, since these split easily into sheets.

Slates

HIDDEN CRYSTALS
Pyrite nodules are common in chalk areas. They may develop interesting shapes. The dull outside breaks to reveal unexpected, radiating crystals inside.

LOCAL STONES
These pebbles reflect the local geology, all coming from the rocks of the immediate neighborhood of the beach where they were collected. They are metamorphic rocks that have been worn into flat disks.

SHELLY PEBBLES
Empty sea shells are subjected to continuous wave action. In time, the sharp edges of broken shells may become smoothed and form pebbles. These are from a beach in New Zealand.

PRESERVED WAVES
Ripple marks form under water from sand carried by low currents and can be seen on many beaches at low tide. In this specimen from Finland, ripple marks are preserved in sandstone, showing that the same sedimentary processes have been going on for millions of years (pp. 54–55).

AMBER PEBBLES
Amber is the fossil resin of extinct cone-bearing trees that lived thousands of years ago. It is especially common along the Baltic coasts of Russia and Poland.

BLACK SANDS

In areas of volcanic activity, beach sand may contain dark minerals and often no quartz. The olivine sand comes from Raasay, Scotland; the magnetite-bearing sand is from Tenerife, an island off the northwest coast of Africa.

Dark olivine sand

Magnetite-bearing sand

Black volcanic ash beach on north coast of Santorini, Greece

Medium-size coarse pebbles

Small, fine pebbles

Finest pebbles

Quartz sand

DISCOVERED IN CHALK

Because flint nodules are hard, they resist abrasion (scraping) and can be seen on beaches in chalk areas, such as those below the famous White Cliffs of Dover, England.

Chalk cliffs often produce pyrite and flint nodules

Smooth, yellowish exterior

Glistening crystals radiate outward

GRANITIC ORIGIN

In granite country, beach pebbles tend to be of quartz, (an abundant vein mineral) or pink or gray granite.

Flint nodules (knobs) from below Chalk cliffs

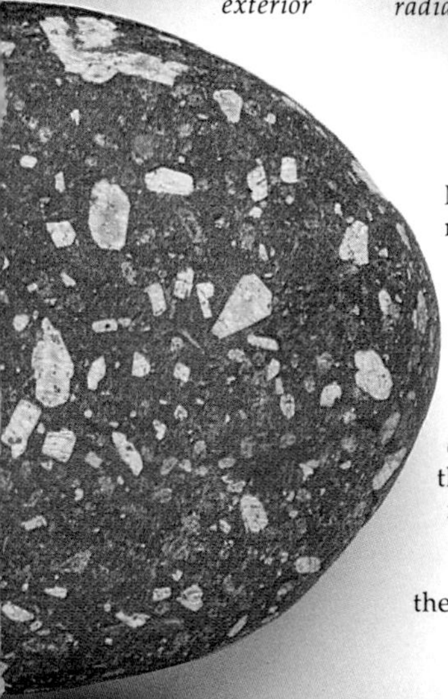

FOREIGN MATERIAL

Not all beach rocks are from local areas. This porphyritic igneous rock was probably carried across the North Sea from Norway to England by ice during the last Ice Age, c. 18,000 B.C.

Assorted glass pebbles

Brick pebble

SYNTHETIC PEBBLES

Apart from the usual natural minerals and rocks, man-made objects may be washed ashore, possibly from ships, or dumped on the beach. Some of them may eventually become rounded by wave action.

PROTECTING THE BEACH

Man-made jetties keep pebbles and sand from drifting.

Igneous rocks

Basalt needle, St. Helena

THESE ROCKS are formed when molten magma from deep within the Earth's crust and upper mantle cools and solidifies (hardens). There are two types: intrusive and extrusive. Intrusive rocks solidify within the Earth's crust and only appear at the surface after the rocks above them have eroded away. Extrusive rocks are formed when magma erupts from a volcano as lava, then cools at the surface.

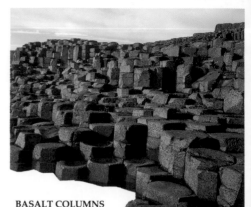

BASALT COLUMNS
When basaltic lava cools, it often forms hexagonal columns. This spectacular example is the Giant's Causeway in Northern Ireland.

Biotite granite

Black grains are biotite, a form of mica (pp. 66–67)

Graphic granite

Long, angular quartz crystals look like ancient writing against the larger pale pink feldspar crystals

Pink granite

Pink coloring due to the high level of potassium feldspar in the rock

GRANITE
A very common intrusive rock, granite consists mainly of coarse grains of quartz, feldspar, and mica (pp. 44–45). The individual grains are large because they form as the magma cooled slowly deep in the earth. Granite is usually speckled and varies in color from gray to red according to the different amount of minerals. Granite is found in many parts of the world. The biotite granite shown here comes from Hay Tor, an outcrop at the the highest point on Dartmoor in southwest England (pp. 46–47).

PITCHSTONE
Formed when volcanic lava cools very quickly, pitchstone contains some small crystals of feldspar and quartz and has a dull, resin-like appearance. Pitchstone may be brown, black, or gray, and large crystals of feldspar and quartz are sometimes visible.

OBSIDIAN
Like pitchstone, obsidian is a glass formed from rapidly cooled lava. It forms so quickly that there is no time for crystals to grow. The sharp edges shown on this sample from Iceland are characteristic of obsidian, hence its use as an early tool.

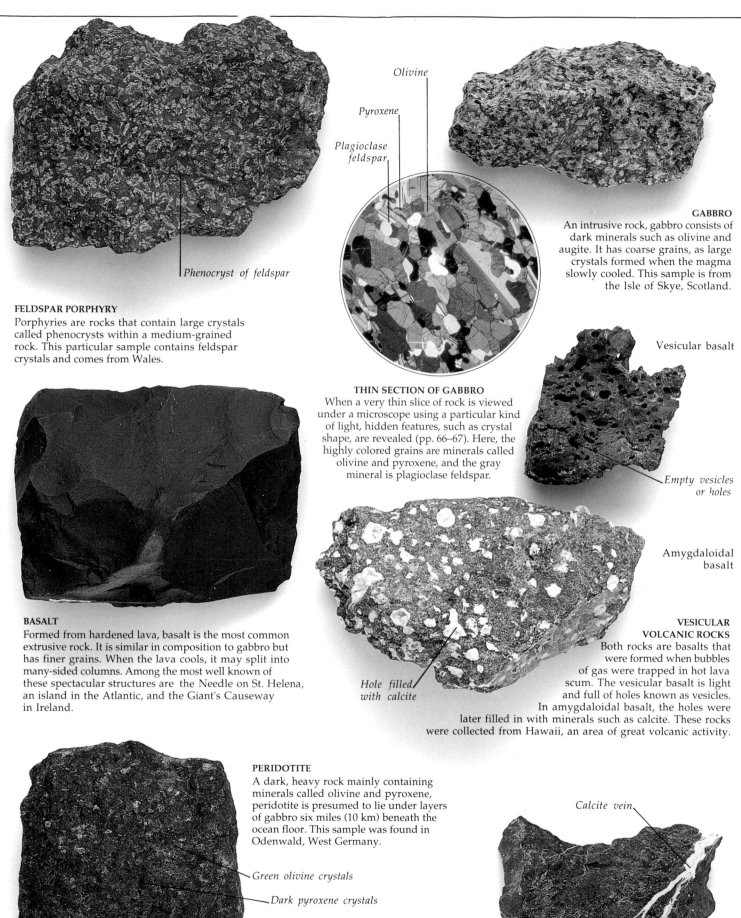

Olivine

Pyroxene

Plagioclase
feldspar

Phenocryst of feldspar

FELDSPAR PORPHYRY
Porphyries are rocks that contain large crystals
called phenocrysts within a medium-grained
rock. This particular sample contains feldspar
crystals and comes from Wales.

GABBRO
An intrusive rock, gabbro consists of
dark minerals such as olivine and
augite. It has coarse grains, as large
crystals formed when the magma
slowly cooled. This sample is from
the Isle of Skye, Scotland.

THIN SECTION OF GABBRO
When a very thin slice of rock is viewed
under a microscope using a particular kind
of light, hidden features, such as crystal
shape, are revealed (pp. 66–67). Here, the
highly colored grains are minerals called
olivine and pyroxene, and the gray
mineral is plagioclase feldspar.

Vesicular basalt

Empty vesicles
or holes

Amygdaloidal
basalt

BASALT
Formed from hardened lava, basalt is the most common
extrusive rock. It is similar in composition to gabbro but
has finer grains. When the lava cools, it may split into
many-sided columns. Among the most well known of
these spectacular structures are the Needle on St. Helena,
an island in the Atlantic, and the Giant's Causeway
in Ireland.

Hole filled
with calcite

**VESICULAR
VOLCANIC ROCKS**
Both rocks are basalts that
were formed when bubbles
of gas were trapped in hot lava
scum. The vesicular basalt is light
and full of holes known as vesicles.
In amygdaloidal basalt, the holes were
later filled in with minerals such as calcite. These rocks
were collected from Hawaii, an area of great volcanic activity.

PERIDOTITE
A dark, heavy rock mainly containing
minerals called olivine and pyroxene,
peridotite is presumed to lie under layers
of gabbro six miles (10 km) beneath the
ocean floor. This sample was found in
Odenwald, West Germany.

Green olivine crystals

Dark pyroxene crystals

Calcite vein

SERPENTINITE
As its name suggests, the dominant
mineral in this coarse-grained red and
green rock is serpentine. It is streaked
with white veins of calcite. Serpentinite
is common in the Alps.

Volcanic rocks

Ejection of lava from Eldfell, Iceland, in 1973

ROCKS THAT ARE FORMED by volcanic activity can be divided into two groups: pyroclastic rocks, and acid and basic lavas. Pyroclastic rocks are formed from either solid rock fragments or bombs of lava blown out of the throat of a volcano. The bombs solidify as they fly through the air. Rocks formed from hardened lavas vary according to the type of lava. Acid lavas are thick and sticky, flow very slowly, and form steep-sided volcanoes. The more fluid, basic lavas form flatter volcanoes or may well up through cracks in the sea floor. Basic lavas are fast-flowing and so quickly spread out to cover vast areas.

Pyroclastic rocks

Pyroclastic means "fire-broken," an apt name for rocks that consist of rock and lava pieces that were blown apart by exploding gases.

Agglomerate formed close to a vent

VOLCANIC BOMBS
When blobs of lava are thrown out of a volcano, some solidify in the air, landing on the ground as hard "bombs." Bombs can be round or irregular. These two specimens are shaped like footballs.

Intrusion breccia formed within a vent

JUMBLED PIECES
The force of an explosion may cause rocks to fragment. As a result, a mixture of angular pieces often fills the central vent or is laid down close to vents. The fragments form rocks known as agglomerates.

Ash

INSIDE A VOLCANO
Magma flows through a central vent or escapes through side vents. Underground it may form dikes that cut across rock layers, and sills of hardened magma parallel to rock layers.

Vent

Side vent

Magma

Sill

Dike

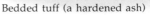

Bedded tuff (a hardened ash)

WIND-BLOWN PARTICLES
Tiny fragments of volcanic ash can travel for thousands of miles in the atmosphere. Where it settles and hardens it forms tuff. This ash erupted from Mount St. Helens, Washington, in 1980. The coarse grains were blown three miles (five km) from the crater; the fine particles were carried by the wind for 17 miles (27 km).

Eruption of Mount St. Helens, 1980

Acid lavas

Thick, sticky acid lavas move slowly and may harden in the volcano's vent, thereby trapping gases. As pressure builds up, the gases may explode to form pyroclastic rocks.

ERUPTION OF VESUVIUS
The famous eruption in A.D. 79 produced a *nuée ardente*, a fast-moving cloud filled with magma and ash. The Roman town of Pompeii was destroyed in this event.

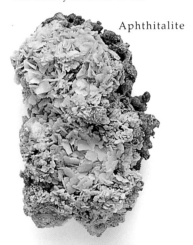

Aphthitalite

Aphthitalite

ROCKS FROM GASES
Inactive volcanoes are said to be "dormant." Even when volcanoes are dormant or dying, volcanic gases may escape and hot springs form. These colorful rocks were formed in this way at Vesuvius.

FLOATING ROCKS
Pumice is hardened lava froth. Because the froth contains bubbles of gas, the rock is peppered with holes, like a honeycomb. Pumice is the only rock that floats in water. This sample is from the Lipari Islands, Italy.

CARAMEL-LIKE LAVAS
This light-colored, fine-grained rock is called rhyolite. The distinctive bands formed as the thick, sticky lava flowed for short distances.

NATURAL GLASS
Although chemically the same as pumice, obsidian (pp. 50–51) has a totally different glassy texture. Because of its sharp edges, early people used it for tools, arrowheads, and ornaments.

Basic lavas

These lavas flow smoothly, and may cover vast distances with a thin layer. As a result, the vent does not get choked and gases can escape, so that although there is plenty of lava, few pyroclastic rocks are formed.

RUNNY LAVAS
Basaltic lavas are fast-flowing and spread out quickly to cover vast areas. This specimen of basalt (pp. 50–51) was deposited by the Hualalai Volcano, one of the many volcanoes on Hawaii.

DESTRUCTION OF AKROTIRI
This town on Santorini, Greece, was buried by volcanic ash, c. 1450 B.C.

WRINKLED ROCKS
When lava flows, the surface cools and forms a skin, which wrinkles as the fluid center keeps on flowing. The resulting rocks are called ropy lavas.

MULTI-COLORED BASALT
Sparkling points in this basalt include green olivine and black pyroxene crystals.

Sedimentary rocks

WHEN ROCKS are weathered and eroded (pp. 46–47) they break down into smaller pieces of rock and minerals. This material, called sediment, may eventually be carried to a new site, often in the sea or in river beds. The sediments are deposited in layers which become buried and compacted (pressed down). In time the particles are cemented together to form new rocks, known as sedimentary rocks. In large outcrops it is often possible to see the various layers of sediment with the naked eye.

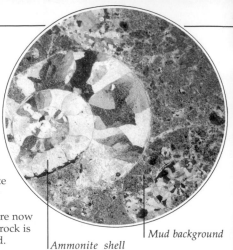

THIN SECTION OF LIMESTONE
Under the microscope (pp. 66–67), fine details in this ammonite limestone are revealed. The ammonite shells (pp. 20–21) show up clearly against the mud background. Ammonites are now extinct, and we know this rock is about 160 million years old.

Ammonite shell

Mud background

RAW INGREDIENTS *above*
Foraminifera are marine organisms that discharge lime. Although rarely bigger than a pinhead, they play an extremely important part in rock building. When they die the shells fall to the ocean floor, where they eventually become cemented into limestone.

Shell remains embedded in rock

Chalk

Oolitic limestone

Shelly limestone

Gastropod limestone

Remains of gastropod shell

Rounded grains known as ooliths

FLINT
A form of silica (pp. 66–67), lumps of flint are often found in limestones, especially chalk. They are gray or black, but the outside may be covered in a white powder-like material. Like obsidian (pp. 50–51), when flint is broken, it has a "conchoidal" fracture (pp. 68–69).

LIMESTONES
Many sedimentary rocks consist of the remains of once-living organisms. In some, such as these shelly and gastropod limestones, the remains of animals are clearly visible in the rock. However, chalk, which is also a limestone, is formed from the skeletons of tiny sea animals that are too small to see with the naked eye. Another limestone, oolite, forms in the sea as calcite builds up around grains of sand. As the grains are rolled backward and forward by waves, they become larger.

ALGAL LIMESTONE
So-called "muddy" limestones like this are often referred to as landscape marbles. This is because when the minerals crystallize they may produce patterns in the shape of trees and bushes.

Hole-filled, irregular-shaped rock

CALCAREOUS TUFA
This extraordinary looking porous rock is formed by the evaporation of spring water and is sometimes found in limestones caves (pp. 56–57).

EVAPORITES
Some sedimentary rocks are formed from the evaporation of saline waters. Examples of these include gypsum and halite. Halite is also known as rock salt, from which we get table salt. Gypsum is used to make plaster of Paris, and in its massive form is called alabaster. Both halite and gypsum are minerals that can be found in large deposits worldwide at sites where evaporation of sea water has occurred.

Gypsum crystals growing from a central point like daisy petals

Single crystals of rock salt are not found as often as massive samples

Halite

Gypsum

Reddish cast caused by impurities in the salt

THE GRAND CANYON
This spectacular scenery was formed by the erosion of red sandstone and limestone.

Grit

Red sandstone

SANDSTONES
Although both these rocks are made by the cementing together of grains of sand, their texture varies. The red sandstone was formed in a desert, where the quartz grains were rounded and polished by the wind. The grains in grit are more angular, as they were buried quickly, before they could be smoothed by rubbing.

CLAY
Formed of very fine grains that cannot be seen by the naked eye, clay feels sticky when wet. It may be gray, black, white, or yellowish. When it is compacted and all the water forced out of it, it forms hard rocks called mudstone or shale.

BEDDED VOLCANIC ASH
In many sedimentary rocks it is possible to see the individual layers of sediments because they form visible bands. Here, the stripes are layers of volcanic ash. The surface has been polished to highlight this feature.

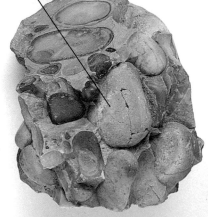

Flint pebble

CONGLOMERATE
The flint pebbles in this rock were rounded by water as they were rolled about at the bottom of rivers or seas. After they were buried, they gradually became cemented together to form a rock known as conglomerate.

Large rock fragment

BRECCIA
Like conglomerate, breccias contain fragments of rock. However, these are much more angular because they have not been rounded by water or carried far from their original home - often the scree (broken rocks) at the bottom of cliffs.

Limestone caves

SPECTACULAR CAVES lined with dripping stalactites and giant stalagmites are perhaps the best known of limestone wonders. The caves are formed when rainwater, a weak acid, dissolves calcium carbonate (calcite or lime) out of limestone, a sedimentary rock (pp. 54–55). In addition to caves, this process also produces several other characteristic features including limestone pavements and special landscapes.

Top section attached to roof of cave

Point of intersection

Stalactites of this thickness may take hundreds of years to form

STALACTITES
Stalactites are formed in caves by groundwater containing dissolved lime. The water drips from the roof and leaves a thin deposit as it evaporates. Growing down from the roof, stalactites increase by a fraction of an inch each year and may eventually be many yards long. Where the water supply is seasonal, stalactites may show annual growth rings like those of tree trunks.

Single stalactite formed from two smaller ones growing together

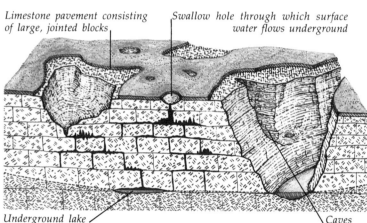

Limestone pavement consisting of large, jointed blocks

Swallow hole through which surface water flows underground

Underground lake

Caves

LIMESTONE LANDSCAPES *above*
Rainwater dissolves calcite in limestone, producing deep, narrow structures ("grikes"). In time, the water dripping down such cracks enlarges them into passages. Although the surface remains dry, flowing water dissolves the rock and produces "swallow holes" at the junctions between grikes. Underground streams flow through caves and form subterranean lakes. Some calcite is redeposited in the caves to form stalactites and stalagmites.

PLAN DE SALES, FRANCE
Limestone pavements consist of large, cracked, flat blocks ("clints") of rock. They occur where weathering of pure limestone leaves nothing behind, such as clay, to make soil.

TUFA
Known as a precipitate, tufa (pp. 54–55) forms when lime is deposited from water onto a rock surface in areas of low rainfall. If a man-made object is left in lime-rich waters it may become coated in tufa.

Coral-like structure

EASE GILL CAVES, ENGLAND
The fine stalactites and stalagmites in this cave form the most spectacular part of a much larger, complex cave system under the hills of the Lancashire Pennines. In fact, this is the largest cave system in Great Britain.

Odd-shaped
stalactite

*Prominent growth
rings mark the gradual
development of the
stalactite as each
deposit formed*

**STONE FOREST,
CHINA**
The staggering
landscape of the
Hunan Province of
China is typical of
karst scenery.
Named after the
limestone area of
Karst in Yugoslavia,
the term is applied
to many limestone
regions, including the
Cumberland Plateau,
U.S.A., parts of the
Blue Mountains,
Australia, and the
Causses, France.

*Point onto which
overhead drips fall*

Orange twin
stalactite

Last section to grow

TRAVERTINE TERRACES
Beautiful travertine
terraces are formed
from the precipitation
(separation) of calcite from
hot springs in limestone
areas such as the
Pamukkale Falls in
Turkey. Travertine is
quarried as a decorative
building stone (pp. 60–61).

STALAGMITES
Stalagmites are
formed on the floor
of caves where
water has dripped
from the roof or a
stalactite above.
Like stalactites,
they develop as
water containing
dissolved lime
evaporates.
Stalactites and
stalagmites can
grow together
and meet to form
pillars. These
have been de-
scribed as "organ
pipes," "hanging
curtains," and
"portcullises."

*Color caused by
impurities in the deposit*

Layer of relatively pure calcite

*End attached to
floor of the cave*

INSIDE A STALACTITE
This specimen has been sliced through the center to reveal
colored bands. The different colors show how the stalactite
formed from deposits of lime with varying degrees of purity.
The purest parts are the whitest.

Metamorphic rocks

THESE ROCKS get their name from the Greek words *meta* and *morphe*, meaning "change of form," and are igneous (pp. 50–51) or sedimentary (pp. 54–55) rocks that have been altered by heat or pressure or both. Such conditions can exist during mountain-building processes; buried rocks may then be subjected to high temperatures and may be squeezed or folded, causing minerals in the rocks to recrystallize and new minerals to form. Other metamorphic rocks are formed when rocks surrounding a hot igneous mass are "baked" by the heat.

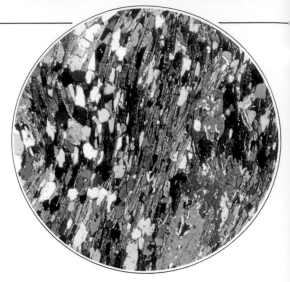

THIN SECTION OF GARNET-MICA SCHIST
Seen through a petrological microscope (pp. 66–67), this Norwegian rock reveals brightly colored, blade-shaped mica crystals. Quartz and feldspar appear as various shades of gray; garnet appears black.

Saccharoidal marble

Evenly sized grains give a sugary appearance

MARBLES
When limestone is exposed to very high temperatures, new crystals of calcite grow and form the compact rock known as marble. It is sometimes confused with quartzite, which looks similar. However, marble is softer and may easily be scratched with a knife. Some medium-grained marble looks sugary and is called saccharoidal. This specimen comes from Korea. The other two marbles are formed from limestone containing impurites, such as pyroxene.

Knobby gray marble

Impure marble

Chiastolite slate

Spotted hornfels

Long chiastolite crystals

Aggregates of carbon

Spotted slate

FROM SLATE TO HORNFELS
The irregular speckles in spotted slate are small groups of carbon crystals, formed by heat from an igneous intrusion. In rocks nearer the intrusion, the temperature is much higher and needle-like crystals of chiastolite form in the slate. The rocks very close to the intrusion become so hot that they completely recrystallize and form a tough new rock called hornfels.

Garnet-muscovite-chlorite schist

Red garnet crystals

Blue, bladelike crystals of kyanite

Kyanite-staurolite schist

SLATE

During mountain building, shale was squeezed so hard that the flaky mineral mica recrystallized at right angles to the pressure. The resulting rock, slate, splits easily into thin sheets.

19th-century slate quarry

SCHISTS

An important group of metamorphic rocks is termed schist. These medium-grained rocks formed from shale or mud but at a higher temperature than slate. For example, the garnet-muscovite-chlorite schist shown here must have been exposed to temperatures of at least 932°F (500°C) because garnet crystals do not grow at lower temperatures. Kyanite-staurolite schist forms under high pressure, 6-9 miles (10-15 km) below the Earth's surface.

Light-colored layer containing quartz and feldspar

Dark band of biotite

Banded gneiss

Black biotite crystals

Blue kyanite crystals

Biotite-kyanite gneiss

ECLOGITE

A rock produced under very high pressure, eclogite is extremely dense and is thought to form in the mantle – considerably deeper than most other rocks. It contains pyroxene and small red crystals of garnet.

Crystals of a green variety of pyroxene

Red garnet crystals

GNEISSES

At high temperatures and pressures, igneous or sedimentary rocks may be changed to gneisses. They have coarser grains than schists and are easy to identify because the minerals often separate into bands. These layers may be irregular where the rock has been folded under pressure.

Dark host rock

Pink granitic rock

MIGMATITE

Under intense heat parts of rocks may start to melt and flow, creating swirling patterns. This is very often shown in migmatites. They are not composed of one rock but a mixture of a dark host rock with lighter colored granitic rock. This sample is from the Scottish Highlands.

Marble

STRICTLY SPEAKING, marble is a metamorphosed limestone (pp. 58–59). However, the term "marble" is often used in the stone industry for a variety of other rocks. All are valued for their attractive range of textures and colors, and because they are easily cut and polished. Marble has been widely used for sculpture, particularly by the ancient Greeks; its use in building reached a peak under the Romans.

IN THE RAW *below*
A true marble, this unpolished, coarsely crystalline specimen of Mijas marble is from Malaga, Spain. Looking at uncut rock, it is hard to imagine the patterns a polished sample will reveal.

MEDICI MADONNA
Michelangelo sculpted this statue from Carrara marble, c. 1530.

CARRARA QUARRY
The world's most famous marble comes from the Carrara quarry in Tuscany, Italy. Michelangelo used it, since it was the local stone.

ITALIAN SPECIALTY *left*
Gray Bardilla marble comes from Carrara, Italy, an area famous for its marble production.

GREEK CONNECTION
Originally from the Greek island of Euboea, streaked Cipollino marble is now quarried in Switzerland, the island of Elba, and Vermont. It was used in the Byzantine church of Saint Sophia in Istanbul, Turkey.

ITALIAN ELEGANCE *right*
Another striking Italian marble is the black and gold variety from Liguria.

TUSCAN STONES
The distinctive texture of the Italian decorative stone *breccia violetto* was the reason for its use in the Paris Opera House in 1875.

TAJ MAHAL
India's most famous monument is made of assorted marbles.

SOUTH AFRICAN SWIRLS
Polished travertine, a variety of tufa (pp. 54–57), has beautiful swirling patterns. This specimen is from Cape Province, South Africa.

SWISS ORIGINS
The limestone breccia known as macchia-vecchia is quarried in Mendrisio, Switzerland.

Detail of marble inlaywork on the Taj Mahal

AFRICAN COPPER *left*
The vivid coloring of green verdite is caused by the presence of copper. It comes from Swaziland, Africa.

ALGERIAN ROCK *bottom*
Breche Sanguine or Red African is a red breccia (pp. 54–55) from Algeria. The Romans used it in the Pantheon, Rome.

Building stones

Quarrying in the early 19th century was still done almost entirely by manual labor

Most of the great monuments of the past – the pyramids, temples, and palaces – have survived because they were made from tough, natural stone. Good building stones must be easy to work but cannot crumble, split, or weather too easily. Today, natural building stones, such as marbles (pp. 60–61), are used mainly as decorative stones, and artificial materials are used for construction.

NUMMULITIC LIMESTONE

This piece of nummulitic limestone was quarried near Cairo, Egypt. It contains small nummulite fossils and was formed about 40 million years ago. The Pyramids were built with stone from the same quarries.

The Pyramids, Egypt, made of local limestone

Fossils

Tooling

PORTLAND STONE

The surface marks on this English limestone are produced by "tooling," a decorative technique that was popular in the last century. After the Great Fire of London in 1666, Portland stone was used to rebuild St. Paul's Cathedral.

OOLITIC LIMESTONE

Some 160 million years old, this limestone is used as a building stone and sometimes in the manufacture of cement.

MOSAIC FLOOR

Small fragments of local stones were often used to make detailed mosaic floors.

Welsh slate

160-million-year-old limestone used for roofing

SLATE

Unlike most building materials, roofing stones must split easily into thin sheets. Slate (pp. 58–59) is ideal. However, where it was not available, builders used local, often inferior, stone for roofing.

NOTRE DAME, PARIS
The famous Parisian cathedral was built of local limestone from the St. Jacques region of Paris between 1163 and 1250. The Paris catacombs (underground tombs) are old quarries.

Interlocking roof tile

Pantile

SANDSTONES
Various colored sandstones make excellent building stones. The French town of Carcassonne is built mostly of sandstone, as are many fine old monuments in India.

Man-made stones

People are now able to manufacture building stone substitutes such as brick and tiles, cement, concrete, and glass. However, all these products originate from rocks of some kind.

230-million-year-old sandstone

GRANITE
Frequently used to cover large buildings, polished granite is also used for gravestones. Much of Leningrad, Russia, including the imperial palaces, is made of imported Finnish granite.

EMPIRE STATE BUILDING, NEW YORK
Although mostly made of granite and sandstone, it contains some man-made materials as well.

ROOFING TILES
In many parts of the world, man-made roofing tiles are molded and fired from clay.

Textured buff brick

Smooth red brick

Red sandstone from Scotland used as a cladding building stone

GREAT WALL OF CHINA
The 4,000-mile (6,400-km) long Great Wall, the largest single structure on Earth, is built of various materials depending on the terrain it passes through. Sections include brick, granite and various local rocks.

BRICKS
Easily molded clays are fired to make bricks. Impurities in clays produce bricks of different colors and strengths, making them good for a number of uses.

CEMENT
Cement is made by grinding and heating a suitable limestone. When mixed with sand, gravel, and water, it produces concrete, perhaps the most common building material today.

Rocks from space

EVERY YEAR about 19,000 meteorites, each weighing over 4 oz (100 g), fall to the Earth. Most fall into the sea or on deserts, and only about five are recovered annually. Meteorites are natural objects that survive their fall from space. When they enter the Earth's atmosphere their surfaces melt and are swept away, but the interiors stay cold. As meteorites are slowed down by the atmosphere, the molten surface hardens to form a dark, thin "fusion" crust.

Fragment of meteorite

Dark, glassy fusion crust formed during passage through Earth's atmosphere

Gray interior consisting mainly of the minerals olivine and pyroxene

PASAMONTE FIREBALL
Photographed by a ranch foreman in New Mexico at 5 A.M., this fireball fell to Earth in March 1933. Meteorites are named after the places where they fall, this one being Pasamonte. The fireball had a low angled path about 500 miles (800 km) long. It broke up in the atmosphere and landed as dozens of meteoritic stones.

EARTH'S CONTEMPORARY *above*
The Barwell meteorite fell at Barwell, Leicestershire, England, on Christmas Eve, 1965. The meteorite is 4.6 billion years old and formed at the same time as the Earth but in a different part of the solar system. Of every ten meteorites seen to fall, eight are stones like Barwell.

METALLIC METEORITE
The Cañon Diablo (Arizona) meteorite collided with the Earth about 20,000 years ago. Unlike Barwell, it is an iron meteorite. These are rarer than stony meteorites and consist of an iron-nickel alloy containing about 5-12 percent nickel. They once formed parts of small asteroids (opposite) which broke up. The largest meteorite known is the Hoba (Namibia, Africa) which is iron and weighs about 60 tons. This cut piece of Cañon Diablo has been polished and partly etched with acid to reveal its internal structure.

METAL AND STONE *below*
"Stony-irons" form a separate group of meteorites. The surface of this slice of the Thiel Mountains meteorite has been cut and polished to show bright metal enclosing stony material, the mineral olivine. It was found in Antarctica where meteorites have been on Earth for about 300,000 years and for much of this time have been encased in ice.

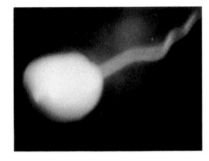

EXPLOSION CRATER
When the Cañon Diablo meteorite hit Arizona, about 15,000 tons of meteorite exploded. It created an enormous hole, Meteor Crater, about 0.75 mile (1.2 km) across and nearly 600 ft (180 m) deep. Only 30 tons of meteorite remained, scattered as small fragments across the surrounding countryside.

Metal

Stony part containing olivine

HALLEY'S COMET
Water-bearing meteorites may have come from comets, such as Halley's - here depicted in the Bayeux tapestry, which tells the story of the Norman Conquest of England in 1066.

ASTEROID STRUCTURE
Many meteorites come from minor planets, or asteroids. They were never part of a single planet, but circle around the sun between the orbits of Mars and Jupiter. The largest asteroid, Ceres, is 632 miles (1,020 km) across. Most asteroids are less than 62 miles (100 km) in diameter. Their interiors consist of a central core of metal, which is the source for some iron meteorites like Cañon Diablo; a core-mantle region which provides stony-iron meteorites like Thiel Mountains; and a crust which provides stony meteorites like Barwell.

Crust

Mantle

Core-mantle

Core

WATER BEARERS
The Murchison meteorite fell in Australia in 1969. It contains carbon compounds and water from space. Material similar to this is believed to form the nucleus of a comet. The carbon compounds were formed by chemical reactions and not by a living organism. Such meteorites are rare - only about three falls in 100 are of this type.

Rocks from the Moon and Mars

Five meteorites found in Antarctica are known to have come from the Moon because they are like lunar highlands rocks collected by the Apollo missions. Eight other meteorites are thought to have come from Mars.

MARTIAN ORIGIN
The Nakhla stone fell in Egypt in 1911 and is reported to have killed a dog. This stone formed 1,300 million years ago, much more recently than most meteorites, and probably came from Mars.

LUNAR DISCOVERIES
The lunar meteorites are made of the same material as the lunar highlands boulder next to Apollo 17 astronaut Jack Schmitt.

MOON ROCK
The Moon's surface is covered with soil made of tiny rock and mineral fragments. It was formed by repeated bombardment of the surface by meteorites. Material like this on the surface of an asteroid was compressed to form many stony meteorites. Here, the light-colored mineral is feldspar, and the darker mineral is pyroxene.

Petrological
microscope

Rock-forming minerals

EIGHT ELEMENTS make up nearly 99 percent of
the Earth's crust. These elements combine to form
naturally occurring minerals. Silicate minerals and
silica form in most common rocks except limestones. Igneous rocks form the
greatest part of the rocky interior of the earth, and specific rock-forming
mineral groups are characteristic of certain types of igneous rocks.

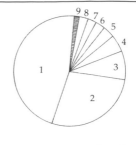

**COMPOSITION OF THE
EARTH'S CRUST**
In weight per cent
order, the elements are:
oxygen (1), silicon (2),
aluminum (3), iron (4),
calcium (5), sodium (6),
potassium (7), mag-
nesium (8), and all
other elements (9).

Minerals in granitic rocks

The minerals that form granitic and dioritic rocks include
feldspars, quartz, micas, and amphiboles. Feldspars are
the most abundant of all minerals and occur in nearly all
types of rock.

*Group of
black
prismatic
crystals with
calcite*

Single
hornblende
crystal

Quartz or
rock crystal

SILICA MINERALS
These include quartz, chalcedony (pp. 102–103), and
opal (pp. 110–111). Quartz is one of the most widely
distributed minerals, found in igneous, sedimentary,
and metamorphic rocks. It is characteristic of
granites, gneisses, and quartzites.

POTASSIC FELDSPARS
Orthoclase is found in many igneous
and metamorphic rocks.
Microcline (the lower-
temperature form
of orthoclase) is
found in granite
pegmatites.

Green microcline
(or amazonstone)
crystal

Twinned crystals of
pink orthoclase

Hornblende, an
amphibole, common in
igneous rocks and in
metamorphic rocks such
as hornblende schists

Tremolite, an amphibole,
common in meta-
morphic rocks

THIN SECTION OF A GRANITIC ROCK
When a slice of diorite about 0.03 mm thick
is viewed under a petrological microscope
(above), it reveals colored amphiboles,
plain gray to colorless quartz, and lined
gray plagioclase feldspar.

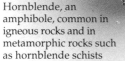

*Silvery, radiating,
needle-like crystals*

Biotite, a dark, iron-
rich mica usually found in
igneous rocks, is also common
in schists and gneisses

AMPHIBOLES
This group of minerals is widely
found in igneous and metamorphic
rocks. Amphiboles can be told apart
from pyroxenes (opposite) by the
characteristic angles between their
cleavage planes (pp. 68–69).

Muscovite, an
aluminum-rich
mica, is abundant
in schists and gneisses

Silvery brown tabular crystals

MICAS
There are two main types of mica: dark
iron- and magnesium-rich mica, and white
aluminium-rich mica. All have perfect
cleavage (pp. 68–69) and split into thin flakes.

Minerals in basic rocks

The seven minerals shown
here are all commonly found
in basic rocks like basalts
and gabbros.

Pink anorthite crystals, a
plagioclase feldspar, with augite

Twinned albite crystals,
a plagioclase feldspar,
with calcite

OLIVINE
This silicate of iron and magnesium is typically
found in silica-poor rocks such as basalts, gabbros,
and peridotites. It often forms as small grains or
large, grainy masses. Clear crystals are cut as
gem peridots (pp. 114–115).

Green olivine crystals

Volcanic bomb containing
olivine, from Vesuvius (pp. 52–53)

Single
crystal of
augite

Nepheline, a
feldspathoid,
with calcite

PLAGIOCLASE
FELDSPARS *above*
This series of
minerals contains
varying amounts
of sodium and
calcium. Plagioclase
feldspars are
common in
igneous rocks.

THIN SECTION OF A BASIC ROCK
A section of olivine basalt in polarized
light reveals brightly colored
olivine, brown-yellow pyroxene,
and minute lined, gray
plagioclase feldspars.

Leucite crystal, a
feldspathoid, on
volcanic rock

FELDSPATHOIDS
As their name suggests, these minerals are related to feldspars, but they contain less silica and
are typically formed in silica-poor volcanic lavas.

Prism-like
crystal of
enstatite
with biotite

Greenish-black
prism-like crystals of
augite, a pyroxene

PYROXENES
The most common pyroxenes
are calcium, magnesium, and
iron silicates. Augite is a common
pyroxene and is found abundantly in
igneous rocks such as gabbros and basalts. Less
common is enstatite, which is found in
gabbros, pyroxenites, and some peridotites.

Other rock-forming minerals

There are two other important
groups of rock-forming
minerals - carbonates
and clays.

CARBONATES
These are import-
ant constituents of
sedimentary
(limestones) or
metamorphic
(marble) rocks,
also in ore vein
deposits. The
most common
is calcite,
the main
ingredient of
limestones.

Dolomite, a carbonate, found in some sedimentary
deposits usually interlayered with limestones

Montmorillonite

Kaolinite (china clay) formed
from partly decomposed orthoclase

Illite

CLAYS
An important part of the sedimentary rock
sequence, clays form from the weathering
and alteration of aluminous silicates. Clays
include kaolinite, montmorillonite, and illite.

The properties of minerals

THE MAJORITY OF MINERALS have a regular crystal structure and a definite chemical composition. These determine the physical and chemical properties that are characteristic for each mineral, some having a great deal of scientific and industrial value. By studying mineral properties such as cleavage, hardness, and specific gravity, geologists can discover how the mineral was formed and use them, along with color and habit (pp. 92–93), to identify minerals.

Structure

Some chemically identical minerals exist in more than one structural state. The element carbon, for example, forms two minerals - diamond and graphite. The difference in their properties is caused by different arrangements of carbon atoms.

Carbon atom

Model of graphite structure

Model of diamond structure | *Carbon atom*

Model showing how one atom is bonded to four others

Diamonds

GRAPHITE
In graphite, a hexagonal mineral formed under high temperature, each carbon atom is closely linked to three others in the same plane. The structure is made of widely spaced layers that are only weakly bonded together. Graphite is one of the softest minerals (Mohs' scale 1-2), and its loose bonding enables it to leave marks on paper, which is why it is used in pencils.

Graphite specimen

DIAMOND
In diamond (pp. 104–105), a cubic mineral formed under high pressure, each carbon atom is strongly bonded to four others to form a tight, rigid structure. This makes diamond extremely hard (Mohs' scale 10). Because of this, it is used as a cutting tool in industry.

Cleavage

When crystals break, some tend to split along well-defined cleavage planes. These are caused by the orderly arrangement of the atoms in the crystal.

Thin layers

THIN SHEETS
Stibnite, an ore of antimony, shows a perfect sheet-like cleavage because of weak bonds between antimony and sulfur atoms.

LEAD STEPS
Galena, the main ore of lead has a perfect cubic cleavage, because of the internal arrangement of lead and sulfur atoms. A broken crystal face consists of many small cubic cleavage steps.

Steps

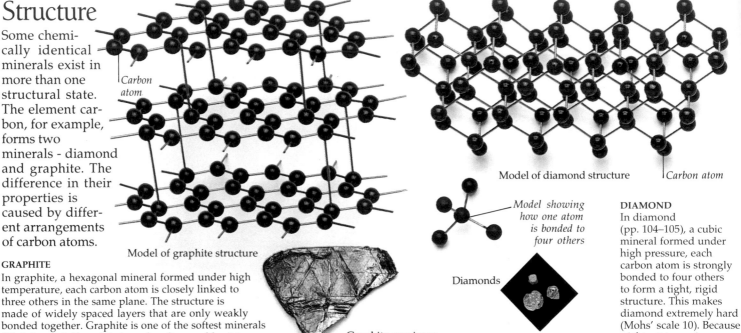

PERFECT BREAK
Barite crystals (pp. 80–81) show an intersecting, perfect cleavage. If this crystal was broken, it would split along these planes of cleavage.

Thin lines show cleavage planes

Smaller crystal growing with larger crystal

PERFECT RHOMB
Any piece of calcite has such a well-developed rhombohedral cleavage that a break in any other direction is virtually impossible.

FRACTURE
Quartz crystals break with a glassy, conchoidal (shell-like) fracture rather than cleaving along any particular plane.

Rounded, conchoidal edges

Hardness

The bonds holding atoms together determine a mineral's hardness. In 1812, the Austrian mineralogist Friedrich Mohs devised a scale of hardness that is still in use today. He selected ten minerals as standards and arranged them so that any mineral on the scale would scratch only those below it. Everyday objects can be used to test where a mineral fits into the scale. A fingernail has a hardness of 2.5, and a penknife is 5.5. Minerals of six and above will scratch glass; glass will scratch apatite and other minerals below it.

GRAPH SHOWING RELATIVE HARDNESS
The intervals between the minerals in Mohs' scale are irregular. Diamond is about 40 times harder than talc, and corundum is only nine times as hard.

1	2	3	4	5	6	7	8	9	10
Talc	Gypsum	Calcite	Fluorite	Apatite	Orthoclase	Quartz	Topaz	Corundum	Diamond

Magnetism

Only two common minerals, magnetite and pyrrhotite (both iron compounds), are strongly magnetic. Some specimens of magnetite called "lodestones" were used as an early form of compass.

NATURAL MAGNET
Magnetite is permanently magnetized and will attract iron filings and other metallic objects such as paper clips.

Clusters of iron filings

Optical properties

As light passes through minerals, many optical effects are produced due to the way light reacts with atoms in the structure.

DOUBLE IMAGE
Light traveling through a calcite rhomb is split into two rays, making a single daisy stalk appear to the eye as two.

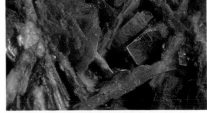

FLUORESCING AUTUNITE
When viewed under ultraviolet light, certain minerals fluoresce (give off light).

Specific gravity

This property relates a mineral's chemical composition to its crystal structure. It is defined as the ratio of the weight of a substance to that of an equal volume of water. Determining the specific gravity may aid identification.

SIZE vs. WEIGHT
The nature of the atoms and the way they are arranged in a mineral determines its specific gravity. These three mineral specimens all weigh the same, but because the atoms in quartz and galena are heavier or more closely packed together than those in mica, the quartz and galena specimens are much smaller.

Mica

Quartz

Galena

Ore minerals and metals

ORE MINERALS are the source of most useful metals. After the ores are mined, quarried, or dredged (from lakes and rivers), they are crushed and separated, then refined and smelted (fused and melted) to produce metal. Even before 5000 B.C., copper was used to make beads and pins. However, it was the Mesopotamians (ancient Arabs) who first began large-scale smelting and casting. Then, around 3000 B.C., tin was added to copper to produce bronze, a harder metal. Still more important was the production of iron, fairly widespread by 500 B.C. Iron was harder than bronze, and iron ores were much more common.

Bronze ritual food vessel from China, c. 10th century BC

Bauxite – aluminum ore (pp. 46–47)

Iron mining, c. 1580

LIGHTWEIGHT ALUMINUM
Aluminum is a good conductor of electricity, lightweight, and not easily corroded. It is used in power lines, building and construction, cars and washing machines, pots and pans.

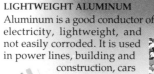

Aluminum kitchen foil

Stacks of aluminum ingots

Hematite - iron ore

TOUGH IRON
Hematite, the most important iron ore, commonly occurs as "kidney ore" - so-called because of its shape. Iron is tough and hard, yet easy to work. It can be cast, forged, machined, rolled, and alloyed with other metals. It is used extensively in the construction industries. Steel and many household items are made from iron.

Steel screw

Rutile - titanium ore

Chalcopyrite - copper ore

STRONG TITANIUM
Rutile and ilmenite are the principal ores of titanium. Usually found in igneous or metamorphic rocks, these two minerals are concentrated by weathering. They form deposits with other minerals, many of which are removed as by-products. Because of its light weight and great strength, titanium is widely used in aircraft frames and engines.

COLORFUL COPPER
Brassy yellow chalcopyrite and bluish-purple bornite are common copper ores. Massive ores are usually found in isolated deposits that are too expensive to mine. Most copper now comes from large, low-grade deposits. Because it is a good conductor, copper is used in the electricity industry, and because it is easy to shape and roll, it is good for household water pipes. It is used in alloys with zinc (brass) and with tin (bronze).

Airliner partially constructed from titanium

Bornite - copper ore

Copper plumbing joint

Galvanized
nail

Sphalerite -
zinc ore

DURABLE NICKEL
Nickel comes from deposits
in large layered gabbroic
intrusions (pp. 50–51) and
from deposits formed by
the weathering of basaltic
igneous rocks. Small
amounts of nickeline
occur in silver and uranium
deposits where nickel is a
by-product. Nickel is used
in alloys like stainless
steel to help it resist
corrosion. High-strength,
high-temperature alloys
are suitable for aircraft
and jet engines.

Nickeline -
nickel ore

Nickel alloy battery

BLACKJACK ZINC
Sphalerite or "black-
jack," as it was
commonly known by
miners, is the most
important zinc ore and
is found in deposits in
sedimentary and
volcanic rocks. Its name
comes from the Greek
word for "deceptive,"
as it has sometimes
been mistaken for other
minerals. Zinc is used
mainly in
"galvanizing,"
whereby sheet steel is
coated with a thin
layer of zinc to prevent
it from rusting.

Zinc processing
in Belgium, c. 1873

Cinnabar - mercury ore

RED MERCURY
The poisonous mercury ore
cinnabar, is found in only a few
locations, those in China, Spain,
and Italy being the best
known. It forms near
volcanic rocks and hot
springs. Mercury is very
dense, has a low melting
point, and is liquid at
room temperature. It is
widely used in the
manufacture of drugs,
pigments, insecticides,
and scientific
instruments, as well
as in dentistry.

Mercury
thermometer

SOFT AND SHINY LEAD
Galena, the main lead ore, is
worked chiefly from deposits in
limestones, such as those in the
southern U.S. Some lead deposits
are mined only because of their
high silver content. Lead is the
densest and softest common metal
and is very resistant to
corrosion, but it is not
very strong. It is used in
storage batteries,
gasoline, engineering,
and plumbing, and
with tin in solder.

Lead solder

Galena -
lead ore

19th-century Cornish
tin mine, England

Crystalline
cassiterite - tin ore

WORKABLE TIN
The tin ore cassiterite is hard, heavy,
and difficult to scratch. Crystalline
forms, like this Bolivian specimen,
are relatively rare. Tin has a low
melting point and does not corrode
easily. It is nonpoisonous, easy to
shape, and a good conductor of
electricity. It is used in solder and
tinplate (although aluminum is now
more widely used for canning). Pewter
is an alloy with roughly 75 percent
tin and 25 percent lead.

Tin can

Precious metals

GOLD, SILVER, AND PLATINUM are crystalline, but single crystals are rarely found. Gold and silver were among the earliest metals worked, over 5,000 years ago. Platinum was first noted in 1735 as a white metal used by the Chibcha Indians of Colombia, and today it is more valuable than gold and silver. All three metals are useful because they are relatively soft and easy to work. They are difficult to destroy and have high SGs (pp. 88–89).

CALIFORNIA GOLD RUSH
The desire for gold has driven people to inhabit areas of the earth from the frozen Arctic to the scorching desert. Gold seekers rushed to California in 1848 and many became rich. Most of the gold was recovered from placer deposits by panning (p. 95).

WELL PLACED
These are deposits of erosion debris from gold-bearing rock. Small particles of gold can be recovered from placer deposits by washing away the sand and gravel.

Gold

Gold is used as a standard against which wealth is measured. Pure gold is a dense (SG=19.3) but soft (H=2.5–3) metal. Before it can be used it has to be refined, and for most uses it is alloyed with other metals to make it harder. Purity of gold for jewelry is measured in carats, pure gold being 24 carats.

GOLD SANDWICH
Gold is sometimes found concentrated in veins and associated with quartz. A wafer-thin layer of crystalline gold can be seen in this quartz vein from New Zealand.

EXCELLENT NUGGET
This fine crystalline gold nugget is known as the Latrobe nugget. It was found in 1855 in the presence of His Excellency C. J. Latrobe, the governor of what was then the colony of Victoria, Australia. Large nuggets of gold are rare.

WORTH ITS WEIGHT
The famous golden Buddha of Bangkok is 5.5 tonnes of solid gold. It is worth over $50 million and is the most valuable religious item in the world.

BUILT ON GOLD
Between 1700 and 1900, the Asante kingdom dominated the area of Africa now known as Ghana. Its power was mostly founded upon its gold resources. Gold dust was the currency for internal trade. This lion ring is from the Asante kingdom.

RARE SIGHT
It is usual for gold to occur as fine grains scattered throughout a rock, or as invisible gold that cannot be seen by the naked eye. This group of crystals from Zimbabwe is therefore extremely rare.

Platinum

Platinum plays a key role in modern technology. It is used as a standard weight, for surgical instruments, and of course in jewelry. The name is derived from *platina*, meaning little silver. Platinum is often found in granules or small nuggets in placer deposits. There are major deposits in the USSR, Canada, and S. Africa but most are of very low concentration.

ROUNDED
Platinum is quite soft (H=4–4.5) so it is unusual to find sharp crystals. These cubic crystals come from Sierra Leone (West Africa).

CROWN OF PLATINUM
The crown of Queen Elizabeth the Queen Mother is made of platinum. It is part of the British Crown Jewels.

RICH LAYER
This piece of platinum-bearing pyroxenite comes from a layer of igneous rock in South Africa called the Merensky reef. This layer is only about 12 in (30 cm) thick but is very rich in platinum.

UNUSUALLY LARGE
Nuggets of platinum are not often as large as this one from the Ural Mountains, USSR. It weighs 2.4 lb (1.1 kg).

MEDIEVAL MINE
In medieval times the area around Sainte Marie, Alsace, France, was one of the richest silver-mining areas in Europe. This illustration from a medieval manuscript shows miners removing silver ore from one of the mines.

Silver

Crystals of silver are rare, but cubic crystals are occasionally found. Silver usually occurs massive or as thick wiry aggregates. In medieval times, silver was more valuable than gold. It was the main metal used for money and was also used for fine metalwork, having a hardness of only 2.5–3. Today, metallic silver is used in electronics, silver plating, and jewelry, and a huge amount is used in the photographic industry (p. 125).

IN NEED OF A POLISH
This dendritic growth (p. 93) of silver crystals is slightly tarnished. It comes from the Huantajaya mines, in Chile.

SILVER WIRE
One of the most famous localities for silver was Kongsberg in Norway. These thick wirelike crystals of silver, with white crystals of quartz and calcite, are from Kongsberg.

VALUABLE BONUS
Silver is now mostly extracted as a by-product from the mining of copper and lead-zinc deposits such as galena, a lead sulfide. These fine crystals of galena come from Silvermines in Ireland.

Cutting and polishing stones

THE EARLIEST METHOD of fashioning stones was to rub one against another to produce a smooth surface that could then be engraved. Much later, professional craftsmen (lapidaries) became skilled at cutting precious stones to obtain the best optical effect and to maximize the size of the cut stone. In recent years, amateur lapidaries have shaped rounded "pebbles" of various minerals by going back to the process of rubbing stones together, using a rotating drum.

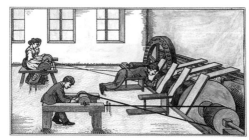

Grinding and polishing agates in a German workshop, c. 1800

Cutting gems

When mined, many gemstones look dull (pp. 102–107). To produce a sparkling gem, the lapidary must cut and polish the stone to bring out its natural beauty, bearing in mind the position of any flaws.

THE HARDEST CUT
Rough diamonds are marked with India ink before cutting.

POPULAR CUTS
The first gemstones were cut into relatively simple shapes, such as the table cut, and cabochon cut. Later lapidaries experimented with more complex faceted cuts, such as the step cut for colored stones, and the brilliant for diamond and other colorless stones.

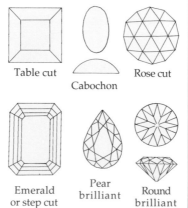

Table cut

Cabochon

Rose cut

Emerald or step cut

Pear brilliant

Round brilliant

Hollow drum

Lid of drum

Belt driven by motor

Rollers

TUMBLING
A tumbling machine is an electrically driven hollow drum mounted on rollers. Mineral fragments are tumbled in the drum with coarse grit and water for about a week. This is repeated with finer grits until the pebbles are rounded and polished.

TUMBLING ACTION
As the drum rotates, pebbles are smoothed and rounded by the grit and by each other.

Rough mineral pieces ready for tumbling

Water added with grits

GRITS AND POLISHES
Various grinding grits are used in sequence from the coarsest to the finest, followed by a polishing powder.

Coarse grinding grit used in first tumbling

Fine grinding grit used for second tumbling

Cerium oxide, very fine polishing powder, used finally to make pebbles smooth and sparkling

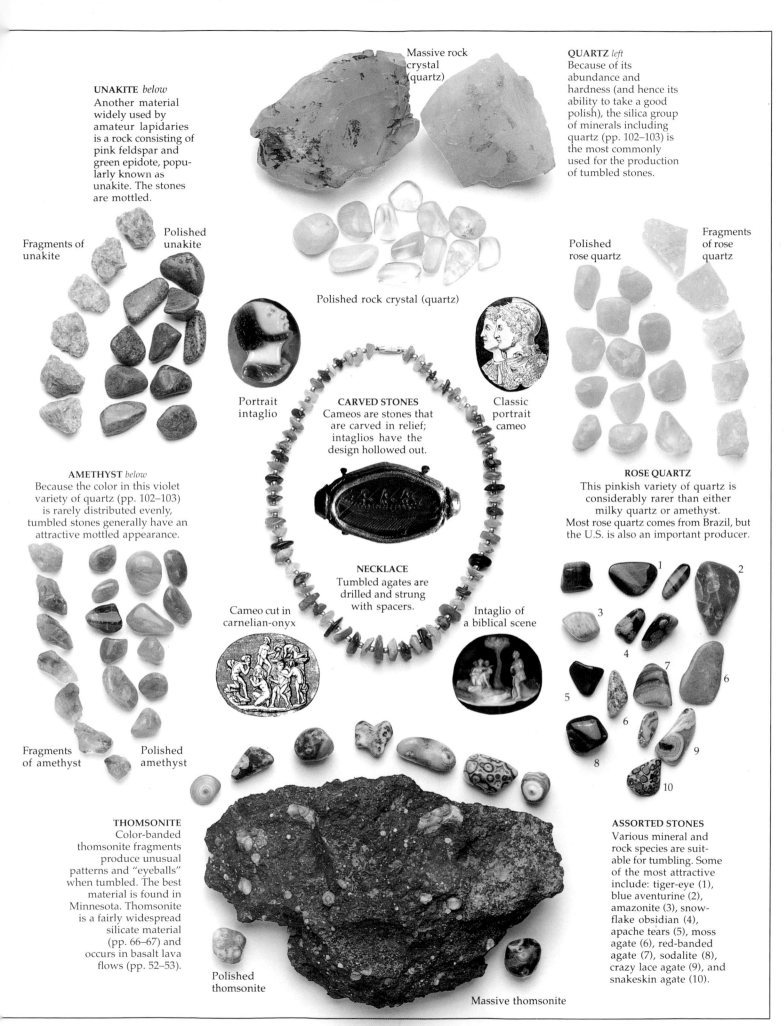

UNAKITE *below*
Another material widely used by amateur lapidaries is a rock consisting of pink feldspar and green epidote, popularly known as unakite. The stones are mottled.

Fragments of unakite

Polished unakite

Massive rock crystal (quartz)

QUARTZ *left*
Because of its abundance and hardness (and hence its ability to take a good polish), the silica group of minerals including quartz (pp. 102–103) is the most commonly used for the production of tumbled stones.

Polished rock crystal (quartz)

Polished rose quartz

Fragments of rose quartz

Portrait intaglio

CARVED STONES
Cameos are stones that are carved in relief; intaglios have the design hollowed out.

Classic portrait cameo

AMETHYST *below*
Because the color in this violet variety of quartz (pp. 102–103) is rarely distributed evenly, tumbled stones generally have an attractive mottled appearance.

ROSE QUARTZ
This pinkish variety of quartz is considerably rarer than either milky quartz or amethyst. Most rose quartz comes from Brazil, but the U.S. is also an important producer.

NECKLACE
Tumbled agates are drilled and strung with spacers.

Cameo cut in carnelian-onyx

Intaglio of a biblical scene

Fragments of amethyst

Polished amethyst

THOMSONITE
Color-banded thomsonite fragments produce unusual patterns and "eyeballs" when tumbled. The best material is found in Minnesota. Thomsonite is a fairly widespread silicate material (pp. 66–67) and occurs in basalt lava flows (pp. 52–53).

Polished thomsonite

Massive thomsonite

ASSORTED STONES
Various mineral and rock species are suitable for tumbling. Some of the most attractive include: tiger-eye (1), blue aventurine (2), amazonite (3), snow-flake obsidian (4), apache tears (5), moss agate (6), red-banded agate (7), sodalite (8), crazy lace agate (9), and snakeskin agate (10).

What is a crystal?

CRYSTALS ARE ASSOCIATED WITH PERFECTION, transparency, and clarity. Many crystals fit these ideals, especially those cut as gemstones, but most are neither perfect nor transparent. Crystals are solid materials in which the atoms are arranged in a regular pattern (pp. 84–85). Many substances can grow in characteristic geometric forms enclosed by smooth plane surfaces. They are said to have crystallized, and the plane surfaces are known as faces. The word *crystal* is based on the Greek word *krystallos*, derived from *kryos*, meaning icy cold. In ancient times it was thought that rock crystal, a colorless variety of quartz, was ice that had frozen so hard it would never melt.

STATES OF MATTER
A material can exist as a solid, a liquid, or a gas depending on its temperature. Water is made of atoms of hydrogen and oxygen bound together to form molecules. In the vapor (steam) the molecules move about vigorously; in the liquid they move slowly; in the solid (ice) they are arranged in a regular order and form a crystalline solid. These ice crystals are about 450 times their real size.

FAMILIAR FACES
These magnificent crystals have formed from hot watery solutions within the earth. They show characteristic faces.

Tourmaline crystal

Quartz crystal

Albite crystals

CRYSTAL MINORITY
Most crystals in this book are of naturally occurring, solid, inorganic materials called minerals. But inorganic compounds not found naturally as minerals also form crystals, such as this artificially grown crystal of potassium magnesium sulfide.

MASSIVE MINERAL
Crystals only grow large and perfect in the right conditions. Most grow irregularly and the faces are often difficult to distinguish. This specimen of the mineral scapolite consists of a mass of small, poorly formed crystals. Minerals in this form are described as massive.

GLASS HOUSE
The Crystal Palace was built for the Great Exhibition of London of 1851, but was destroyed by fire in 1936. The roof and outer walls were made of nearly 300,000 panes of glass – not crystals.

Pyrolusite dendrites

CRYSTAL LINING
These fern-like growths look like a plant but are in fact crystalline growths of the mineral pyrolusite. Such crystals are called dendrites (pp. 90–91) and are often found lining joints and cracks in rocks.

Cut heliodor

18th-century miniature painting of an Indian woman bedecked with jewelry

GEM OF A CRYSTAL
Most gemstones are natural crystals chosen for their beauty, durability, and, in many instances, rarity. They are usually cut and polished (pp. 74–75). Crystals with the same composition and properties as naturally occurring minerals can now be grown artificially (pp. 96–97) and cut as gemstones.

Cut aquamarine

MOST IRREGULAR
Some of the objects which we know as "crystal" are glass and are not truly crystalline. Glass has little structure, as it is cooled too quickly for the atoms to arrange themselves into a regular order, and is said to be amorphous.

POTATO SURPRISE
Crystals often occur in places where you would least expect to find them. In certain plowed fields of southern England, irregular nodules (lumps) known as "potato stones" are found. When broken open, they often reveal sparkling crystals.

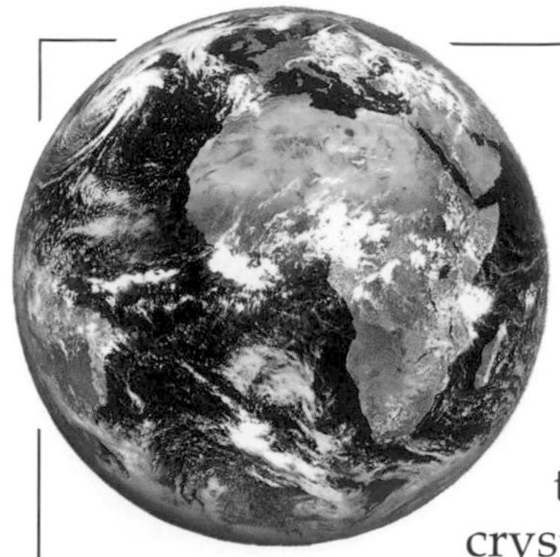

A world of crystals

CRYSTALS ARE ALL AROUND US. We live on a crystal planet in a crystal world. The rocks which form the earth, the moon, and meteorites – pieces of rock from space – are made up of minerials and virtually all of these minerals are made up of crystals. Minerals are naturally occurring crystalline solids composed of atoms and various elements. The most important of these are oxygen, silicon, and six common metallic elements including iron and calcium. Crystalline particles make up mountains and form the ocean floors. When we cross the beach we tread on crystals. We use them at home (pp. 124–125) and at work (pp. 98–99); indeed, crystals are vital to today's technology.

CRYSTAL LAYERS
The earth is formed of three layers: the crust, the mantle, and the core. These are made mostly of solid rock-forming minerals. Some rocks, such as pure marble and quartzite, are made of just one mineral, but most are made of two or more.

Orthoclase

Quartz

Biotite

GRANITE
The most characteristic rock of the earth's outermost layer, the continental crust, is granite. It consists mainly of the minerals quartz, feldspar, and mica. This specimen shows crystals of the feldspar mineral orthoclase, with small crystals of quartz and biotite mica.

ECLOGITE
The earth's upper mantle is probably mostly peridotite but other rocks include dunite and eclogite. This specimen, originally from the mantle, is eclogite containing green pyroxene and small garnets.

Garnet crystal

METEORITE
It is thought that the center of the earth, the inner core, may be similar in composition to this iron meteorite. It has been cut, polished, and acid-etched to reveal its crystalline structure.

LIQUID ROCK
Molten lava from inside the earth can erupt from volcanoes such as the Kilauea volcano, Hawaii, shown here. When the lava cools, minerals crystallize and it becomes a solid rock.

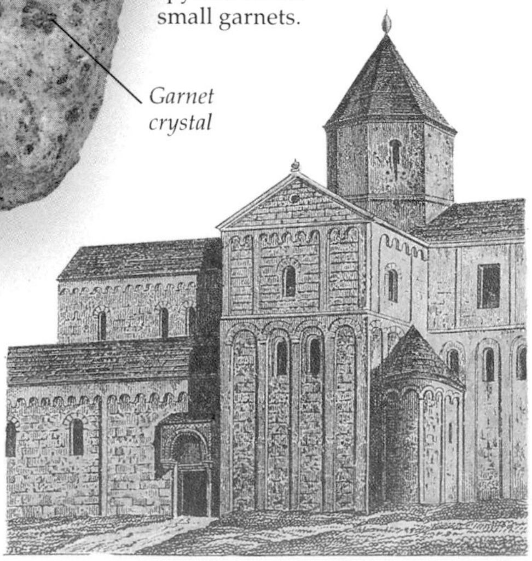

CRYSTAL STRENGTH
Most buildings are made of crystals. Both natural rock and artificial materials are mostly crystalline, and the strength of cement depends on the growth of crystals.

DOWN TO DUST
Pebbles, sand, and the greater part of soil are all formed from eroded rocks. Eventually, they will be eroded even further to form dust in the air (pp. 102–103). Like the rocks they come from, these familiar things are all made up of crystals.

Quartzite pebbles

Basalt pebble

Feldspar crystal

Quartz sand grains

Soil

CRYSTAL CAVE
Fine stalactites and stalagmites form the spectacular scenery in these grottoes of Giita in Lebanon.

DRIP BY DRIP
Stalagmites and stalactites are mostly made of calcite crystals. This group of stalagmites grew upward from the floor of an abandoned mine as water, rich in calcium carbonate, dripped down from above.

Calcite crystals

Organic crystals
Crystals do not only grow in rocks. The elements that make up most rock-forming minerals are also important to life on earth. For example, minerals such as calcite and apatite crystallize inside plants and animals.

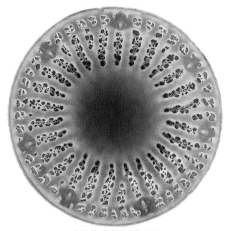

MICROCRYSTALS
This microscope picture of a diatom, *Cyclotella pseudostelligera*, shows a symmetrical (even) structure. Diatoms are microscopic algae whose cell walls are made up of tiny silica crystals.

ANIMAL MINERAL
Gallstones sometimes form inside an animal's gall bladder. This gallstone from a cow has exactly the same crystalline composition as struvite, a naturally occurring mineral.

STRESSFUL
Adrenaline is a hormone, a substance produced by the body to help it cope with stress. This greatly enlarged picture of adrenaline shows it is crystalline.

HUMAN APATITE
Bones contain tiny crystals of the mineral apatite. They make up the skeleton in vertebrate mammals – those that have a backbone, such as humans and horses. This is a human humerus (upper arm bone).

Natural beauty

WELL-FORMED CRYSTALS are objects of great beauty and extreme rarity. Conditions have to be just right for them to grow (pp. 90–91) and any later changes in conditions must act to protect rather than destroy them. Even if they do grow and survive, many are destroyed by people during mining and other activities. Survivors are therefore of great interest. The crystals shown are about 60 percent of their real size.

PROUSTITE
Crystals of cherry-red proustite are known as ruby silvers and are often found along with silver deposits. This exceptional group was collected from a famous silver mine area at Chanarcillo, Copiapo, Chile. The mines were extensively worked between 1830 and 1880.

BOURNONITE
These magnificent bright-gray "cogwheel" crystals were collected from the Herodsfoot lead mine in Cornwall, England. Between 1850 and 1875 this mine produced bournonite crystals of a quality still unsurpassed elsewhere.

Crystal Dream
a science fiction creation which the French artist Jean Giraud, known as Moebius, based on crystal shapes

Giant rock crystal and smoky quartz crystal, as found inside cavities in certain rocks, especially in Brazil

EPIDOTE
This is one of the finest epidote crystals known, as it shows good color and fine prismatic habit (pp. 92–93) for a crystal of this species. It was collected from a small mine high in the mountains in Austria. The mineral site was said to have been discovered by a mountain guide in 1865.

BARITE
The iron mining areas of Cumbria, England, are renowned for the quality of their barite crystals. The crystals display a range of colors, and each color comes mostly from one mine. These golden-yellow crystals came from the Dalmellington mine, Frizington, where many fine specimens were collected during the 19th century.

TOPAZ
This perfect topaz crystal was one of many wonderful crystals that were found in the last century close to the Urulga River in the remote areas of the Borshchovochnyy Mountains in Siberia. Most were yellowish brown and some weighed up to 22 lb (10 kg).

BENITOITE
These triangular-shaped, sapphire-blue crystals of benitoite (pp. 118–119) were found close to the San Benito River in California. Such crystals have not been found in this quantity anywhere else in the world.

CALCITE
One of the most common and widely distributed minerals is calcite. It occurs as crystals in many different shapes and shades of color. Some of the most beautiful calcite crystal groups came from the Egremont iron mining area of Cumbria, England, in the late 19th century. This typical example consists of many fine colorless crystals, some of which are slightly tinged with red.

Beautifully formed beryl crystals from various parts of the world

Crystals – outside ...

IN CONTACT
A contact goniometer is used to measure the angles between crystal faces. The law of constancy of angle states that in all crystals of the same substance, the angles between corresponding faces are always the same.

Scale from which interfacial angle is read

Topaz crystal in position for measuring

Romé de l'Isle (1736-90), who established the law of constancy of angle first proposed by the scientist Steno in 1669

A WELL-FORMED CRYSTAL has certain regular or symmetrical features. One feature is that sets of faces have parallel edges. Another feature of many crystals is that for every face, there is a parallel face on the opposite side. Crystals may have three types of symmetry. If a crystal can be divided into two, so that each half is a mirror image of the other, the line that divides them is called a "plane of symmetry." If a crystal is rotated around an imaginary straight line and the same pattern of faces appears a number of times in one turn, then the line is an "axis of symmetry." Depending on how many times the pattern appears, symmetry around an axis is described as twofold, threefold, fourfold, or sixfold. If a crystal is entirely bounded by pairs of parallel faces then it has a "center of symmetry."

Cubic system represented by galena. Essential symmetry element: four threefold axes.

SEVEN SYSTEMS
Crystals have differing amounts of symmetry and are placed, according to this, in one of seven major categories called systems. Crystals in the cubic system have the highest symmetry. The most symmetrical have 9 planes, 12 axes, and a center of symmetry. Crystals in the triclinic system have the least symmetry with only a center of symmetry or no symmetry at all.

Tetragonal system represented by idocrase. Essential symmetry element: one fourfold axis.

Orthorhombic system represented by barite. Essential symmetry element: three twofold axes.

Crystal in position for measuring

ON REFLECTION
Made in about 1860, this optical goniometer is designed to measure the interfacial angles of small crystals by the reflection of light from their faces. The crystal is rotated until a reflection of light is seen from two adjacent faces. The angle between the two faces is read off the graduated circle on the right.

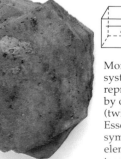

Monoclinic system represented by orthoclase (twinned). Essential symmetry element: one twofold axis.

Triclinic system represented by axinite. No axis of symmetry.

Hexagonal system represented by beryl. Essential symmetry: one sixfold axis.

SAME BUT DIFFERENT

Some crystallographers (studiers of crystals) consider the trigonal system part of the hexagonal system. Both systems have the same set of axes, but the trigonal has only threefold symmetry. This is seen in the terminal faces.

Trigonal system represented by calcite. Essential symmetry: one threefold axis.

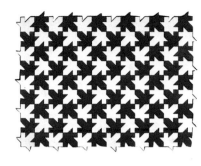

DESIGNED FOR SYMMETRY

This maple leaf design is one of 13 made to commemorate the 13th Congress of the International Union of Crystallography, held in Canada in 1981. The repetitive designs were based on the elements of crystal symmetry.

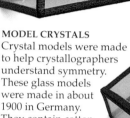

Triclinic model

Cubic model

MODEL CRYSTALS

Crystal models were made to help crystallographers understand symmetry. These glass models were made in about 1900 in Germany. They contain cotton threads strung between the faces to show axes of rotation.

Hexagonal model

Form

Crystals of the same mineral may not look alike. The same faces on two crystals may be different sizes and therefore form different-shaped crystals. Crystals may also grow with a variation of "form." Shown here are three forms found in the cubic crystal system, illustrated by pyrite.

Studies of the transformation of geometrical bodies from Leonardo da Vinci's sketchbook

CUBE

A form of six square faces that make 90° angles with each other. Each face intersects one of the fourfold axes and is parallel to the other two.

OCTAHEDRON

A form of eight equilateral triangular faces, each of which intersects all three of the fourfold axes equally.

PYRITOHEDRON

This form consists of 12 five-sided faces. It is also known as a pentagonal dodecahedron.

Below: Diagram to show the relationship between different cubic forms

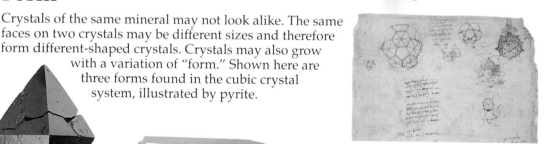

Dodecahedral face

Octahedral face

Cubic face

COMBINATION OF FORMS

These crystals show cubic faces combined with octahedral faces with poorly developed dodecahedral faces blending into the cubic faces.

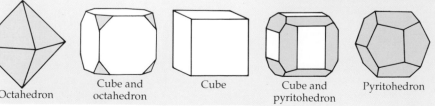

Octahedron

Cube and octahedron

Cube

Cube and pyritohedron

Pyritohedron

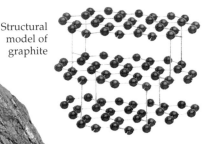
Diamond
set in a
ring

Graphite
pencil

NOT CARBON COPIES
Both diamond and graphite
are formed from the chemical
element carbon, but there are striking
differences in their properties. This is
explained by their different
internal structures.

…and inside

THE INTERNAL ATOMIC STRUCTURE of crystals determines their regular shape and other properties. Each atom has its own special position and is tied to others by bonding forces. The atoms of a particular mineral always group in the same way to form crystals of that mineral. In early crystallography, the study of crystals, one of the most significant deductions was made by R. J. Haüy (p. 85) in 1784. In 1808, English chemist J. Dalton defined his theory that matter was built up from tiny particles called atoms. In 1895, German physicist W. Röntgen discovered X-rays, and in 1912, Laue (p. 85) realized that X-rays might help determine the arrangement of atoms within a solid. This was the start of our understanding of the inside of crystals.

Graphite
crystal

Structural model of
graphite

GRAPHITE
In graphite, carbon atoms are linked in a hexagonal (six-sided) arrangement in widely spaced layers. The layers are only weakly bonded and can slip easily over one another, making graphite one of the softest minerals.

Diamond
crystal

DIAMOND
In diamond, each carbon atom is strongly bonded to four others to form a rigid compact structure. This structure makes diamond much harder than graphite.

Structural model of diamond

Augite crystal

ACTINOLITE
Silicate minerals, present in all common rocks apart from limestone, have a basic unit of a tetrahedron (four faces) of one silicon and four oxygen atoms (SiO_4). Actinolite, a member of a group of minerals known as amphiboles, has a structure based on a double chain of these tetrahedra.

GOLD ATOMS
Crystalline solids have a complex latticework of atoms. This photograph shows the atomic lattice of gold magnified millions of times. Each yellow blob represents an individual atom.

Model showing SiO_4 tetrahedra in a single-chain silicate

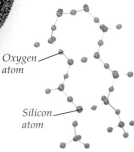
Oxygen atom

Silicon atom

AUGITE
An important group of silicate minerals is the pyroxenes, including augite. Their internal structure is based on a single chain of SiO_4 tetrahedra.

Model showing SiO_4 tetrahedra in a double-chain silicate

BERYL
In some silicate materials, the internal structure is based on groups of three, four, or six SiO_4 tetrahedra linked in rings. Beryl (pp. 108–109) has rings made of groups of six tetrahedra.

MAX VON LAUE (1879–1960)
Laue showed with X-ray photographs that crystals were probably made of planes of atoms.

Wave-length (meters)	
10^{-15}	Gamma rays
10^{-11}	
10^{-9}	X-rays
10^{-7}	Ultraviolet radiation
10^{-6}	Visible light
10^{-4}	Infrared radiation (heat)
1	Microwaves
	Radio waves
10^5	

Decreasing wavelength →

ELECTRO-MAGNETIC WAVES
X-rays are part of the electromagnetic radiation spectrum. All radiations can be described in terms of waves, many of which, such as light, radio, and heat, are familiar. The waves differ only in length and frequency. White light, which is visible to the human eye, is composed of electromagnetic waves varying in wavelength between red and violet in the spectrum (pp. 86–87), but these visible rays are only a fraction of the whole spectrum.

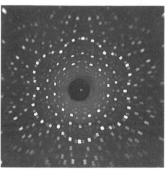

X-RAY PHOTO
This Laue photograph shows the diffraction, or splitting up, of a beam of X-rays by a beryl crystal. The symmetrical pattern is related to the hexagonal symmetry of the crystal.

Cleavage

Some crystals split along well-defined planes called cleavage planes which are characteristic for all specimens of that species. Cleavage forms along the weakest plane in the structure and is direct evidence of the orderly arrangement of atoms.

TOPAZ
This fine blue topaz crystal from Madagascar shows a perfect cleavage. Topaz is one of a group of silicates with isolated SiO_4 groups in their structure.

Cleavage plane

MICA
The micas are a group of silicate minerals which have a sheet structure. The atomic bonding perpendicular (at right angles) to the sheet structure is weak, and cleavage occurs easily along these planes.

Thin cleavage flakes

R. J. HAÜY (1743–1822)
Haüy realized that crystals had a regular shape because of an inner regularity. He had seen how calcite often fractures along cleavage planes into smaller diamond shapes (rhombs) and decided crystals were built up by many of these small, regularly stacked blocks.

QUARTZ
The structure of quartz is based on a strongly bonded, three-dimensional network of silicon and oxygen atoms. Crystals do not cleave easily but show a rounded, concentric fracture known as conchoidal.

The color of crystals

MOONSTONES
The most familiar gem variety of the feldspar minerals is moonstone (pp. 114–115). The white or blue sheen is caused by layers of tiny crystals of albite within orthoclase.

THE COLOR OF A CRYSTAL can be its most striking feature. The causes of color are varied, and many minerals occur in a range of colors. Something looks a particular color largely due to your eye and brain reacting to different wavelengths of light (pp. 84–85). When white light (daylight) falls on a crystal, some of the wavelengths may be reflected, and some absorbed. If some are absorbed, those remaining will make up a color other than white because some of the wavelengths that make up white light are missing. Sometimes light is absorbed and re-emitted without changing and the mineral will appear colorless.

Transparent, colorless rock crystal

Transparent, purple amethyst

Opaque milky quartz

SEE-THROUGH OR OPAQUE
Crystals can be transparent (they let through nearly all the light and can be seen through), translucent (they let some light through but cannot be seen through clearly), or opaque (they do not let any light through and cannot be seen through at all). Most gemstones are transparent but can be colored or colorless.

Idiochromatic

Some minerals are nearly always the same color because certain light-absorbing atoms are an essential part of their crystal structure. These minerals are described as idio-chromatic. For example, copper minerals are nearly always red, green, or blue according to the nature of the copper present.

ISAAC NEWTON (1642–1727)
Sir Isaac Newton was an English scientist who achieved great fame for his work on, among other things, the nature of white light. He discovered that white light can be separated into seven different colors, and followed this with an explanation of the theory of the rainbow.

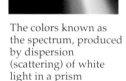

The colors known as the spectrum, produced by dispersion (scattering) of white light in a prism

SULFUR
Sulfur is an idiochromatic mineral and normally crystallizes in bright yellow crystals. These are often found as encrusting masses around volcanic vents and fumaroles (pp. 90–91).

AZURITE
Azurite is a copper mineral which is always a shade of blue – hence the term azure blue. In ancient times it was crushed and used as a pigment.

Allochromatic

A large number of minerals occur in a wide range of colors caused by impurities or light-absorbing defects in the atomic structure. For example, quartz, diamond, beryl, and corundum can be red, green, yellow, and blue. These minerals are described as allochromatic.

RHODOCHROSITE
Manganese minerals such as rhodochrosite are usually pink or red. The bright red color of some beryls is due to tiny amounts of manganese.

ERYTHRITE
Cobalt minerals such as erythrite are usually pink or reddish. Trace amounts of cobalt may color normally colorless minerals.

FLUORITE
When exposed to invisible ultraviolet light (p. 15), some minerals emit visible light of various colors. This is called fluorescence, usually caused by foreign atoms called activators in the crystal structure. The fluorescent color of a mineral is usually different from its color in daylight. This fluorite crystal is green in daylight.

Play of colors

The color in some minerals is really a play of colors like that seen in an oil slick or a soap bubble. This may be produced when a light is affected by the physical structure of the crystals, such as twinning (pp. 90–91) or cleavage planes (pp. 84–85), or by the development during growth of thin films. Microscopic "intergrowths" of plate-like inclusions (pp. 90–91) also interfere with the light.

HEMATITE
The play of colors on the surface of these hematite crystals from Elba is called iridescence. It is due to the interference of light in thin surface films.

SALT
A space in the atomic structure of a crystal, caused by a missing atom, can form a color center. Coloration of common salt is thought to be caused by this.

LABRADORITE
The feldspar mineral labradorite can occur as yellowish crystals, but more often it forms dull gray crystalline masses. Internal twinning causes interference of light, which gives the mineral a sheen, or schiller, with patches of different colors.

Identification

"WHAT IS IT?" This is the first question to ask about a mineral, crystal, or gemstone. In order to identify a crystal it is necessary to test its properties. Most minerals have fixed or well-defined chemical compositions and a clearly identifiable crystal structure (pp. 84–85). These give the mineral a characteristic set of physical properties. Color (pp. 86–87), habit (pp. 92–93), cleavage (pp. 84–85), and surface features can be studied using a hand lens, but in most cases that is not enough for positive identification. Other properties such as hardness and specific gravity (SG) can be studied using basic equipment, but more complex instruments are needed to fully investigate optical properties, atomic structure, and chemical composition.

Sherlock Holmes, the fictional master of criminal investigation and identification, looks for vital clues with the help of a hound

SPOT THE DIFFERENCE
These two gemstones look almost identical in color, yet they are two different minerals: a yellow topaz (*left*), and a citrine (*right*).

SEEING DOUBLE
An important property of some crystals is birefringence, or double refraction, as in this piece of calcite. Light traveling through the calcite is split into two rays, causing a doubled image.

Doubled image of wool seen through calcite

Chemical beam balance being used to determine specific gravity

Orthoclase SG = 2.6   Galena SG = 7.4

WEIGHING IT UP
Specific gravity is a basic property. It is defined as the ratio of the weight of a substance compared to that of an equal volume of water. If W_1 = weight of specimen in air, and W_2 = its weight in water, then W_1 divided by $W_1 - W_2$ = SG. The two crystals shown are of similar size but their SG differs considerably. This reflects the way the atoms are packed together.

Hardness

The property of hardness is dependent upon the strength of the forces holding atoms together in a solid. A scale of hardness on which all minerals can be placed was devised by F. Mohs in 1822. He selected 10 minerals as standards and arranged them in order of hardness so that one mineral could scratch only those below it on the scale. Intervals of hardness between the standard minerals are roughly equal except for that between corundum (9) and diamond (10).

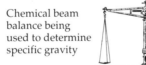

1
Talc

2
Gypsum

3
Calcite

4
Fluorite

PROBING ABOUT
A modern technique called electron probe micro-analysis was used to investigate the specimen on the left. In a scanning electron microscope (SEM) equipped with a special analysis system, a beam of electrons was focused on the specimen, producing a characteristic X-ray spectrum (below).

10
Diamond

The X-ray spectrum showing large peaks for iron (Fe), arsenic (As), calcium (Ca), and zinc (Zn)

MISTAKEN IDENTITY
It is always important to know the chemical composition of a crystal or mineral, and modern techniques can reveal some surprising results. These small blue-gray crystals on limonite were shown by X-ray methods to be the mineral symplesite (hydrated iron arsenate). However, further analysis showed that they unexpectedly contain some calcium and zinc as well.

Ruby colored by chromium

Almandine garnet colored by iron

SHADOW PLAY
Refractive index (RI) is a mineral's refracting ability – that is, its ability to bend a beam of light – and is useful in identification. It can be measured, along with birefringence, with a refractometer. A light is made to pass through the stone, and one or two shadow edges form on a scale depending on whether the gem is singly or doubly refractive. The position of the shadow gives the RI.

ABSORBED IN STONE
A spectroscope is often used to distinguish between gemstones of a similar color. Light enters through a slit and separates into its spectrum of colors (pp. 86–87). If a gemstone is put between the light source and the slit, dark bands appear in the spectrum, where wavelengths have been absorbed by the stone.

Spinel
RI: 1.71

Tourmaline
RI: 1.62 and 1.64

9
Corundum

Diamond

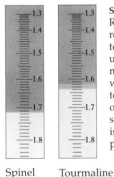
5
Apatite

6
Orthoclase

7
Quartz

8
Topaz

Sapphire

Chrysoberyl

Topaz

Garnet

Opal

Peridot

Amethyst

MOHS (1773-1839)
Friedrich Mohs was professor of mineralogy at Graz, and later Vienna, Austria. While at Graz he developed the scale of hardness.

Natural growth

CRYSTALS GROW as atoms arrange themselves, layer by layer, in a regular, three-dimensional network (pp. 84–85). They can form from a gas, liquid, or solid and usually start growing from a center or from a surface. Growth continues by the addition of similar material to the outer surfaces until the supply stops. It is rare to find a perfect crystal. Temperature, pressure, chemical conditions, and the amount of space all affect growth. It is estimated that in an hour, millions and millions of atoms arrange themselves layer by layer across a crystal face. With this number it is not surprising that defects occur.

TWISTED AROUND
Crystals can be bent or twisted like this stibnite. This may be because they were bent by some outside force during growth.

CRYSTAL LAYERS
This magnified image, called a photomicrograph, shows the layers of different crystals in a thin section of magmatic rock.

Sal ammoniac crystals

MINERAL SPRINGS
Hot watery solutions and gases containing minerals, such as sal ammoniac (ammonium chloride), sometimes reach the earth's surface through hot springs and fumaroles (gas vents). Here, the minerals may crystallize.

IN THE POCKET
Holes in rocks often provide space in which crystals can grow. Cavities containing fine gem-quality crystals are known as gem pockets. This gem pocket at Mt. Mica, Maine, was discovered in 1979.

SETTLING DOWN
As magma (the molten rock below the earth's surface) cools, so crystals of various minerals form. Some magmatic rock forms in layers, as different rock-forming minerals settle and crystallize at different times.

CHANGED BY FORCE
As a result of the high temperatures and pressures deep within the earth's crust, minerals in solid rock can recrystallize, and new minerals form. This process is known as metamorphism. The blue kyanite and brown staurolite crystals in this specimen have been formed in this way.

Siderite

Quartz

Chalcopyrite

TAKING SHAPE
Many minerals crystallize from watery solutions. We only see the final product but can often work out a sequence of events. In this specimen, a fluorite crystal grew first, and was coated with siderite. The fluorite was later dissolved and removed, but the coating of siderite kept the characteristic cubic shape of the fluorite crystal. Lastly, crystals of chalcopyrite and quartz grew inside the hollow cube.

BUILDING BLOCKS
Skyscrapers are built in a similar way to crystals – by adding layer upon layer to the same symmetrical shape.

Twinning

During crystallization, two crystals of the same mineral may develop in such a way that they are joined at a common crystallographic plane. Such crystals are known as twinned crystals. The apparent line of contact between the two parts is known as the twin plane.

Etch pit

BERYL ETCHING
Solutions or hot gases may dissolve the surface of certain crystals after growth, as in this beryl. Regularly shaped hollows known as etch pits are formed. Their shape is related to the internal atomic structure.

SPIRALING AROUND
Crystal faces are rarely flat, due to a variety of growth defects. This magnified image of the surface of a crystal shows the atoms forming a continuous spiral, instead of layers across the crystal face.

BUTTERFLY TWINS
This simple type of twin is known as a butterfly contact twin crystal because of its resemblance to butterfly wings. This example is calcite.

GROWING UP TOGETHER
When the two parts of twin crystals grow into each other, they are known as penetration twins. The example shown is a twin of purple fluorite.

FORM COMPETITION
Many crystals have parallel lines called striations running along or across their faces. These are usually caused when two forms (p. 82) try to grow at the same time.

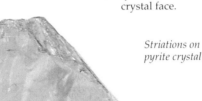

Striations on pyrite crystal

AT THE HOP
Some crystals tend to build up more quickly along the edges of the faces than at the centers, producing cavities in the faces. These are known as hopper crystals and are well illustrated here by crystals of galena.

CRYSTAL ENCLOSURE
During growth, a crystal may enclose crystals of other minerals, commonly hematite, chlorite, and tourmaline. These are known as inclusions.

Rutile inclusions in quartz

Fluid inclusion

PHANTOM QUARTZ
Interruptions in the growth of a crystal can produce regular inclusions. Parallel growth layers, as in this quartz, are sometimes called "phantoms." These layers formed as dark-green chlorite coated the crystal of quartz during several separate breaks in its growth.

"Phantom" growth layers

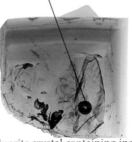

A fluorite crystal containing inclusions of ancient mineral-forming fluids

91

Good habits

TABULAR
This large red crystal of wulfenite comes from the Red Cloud mine in Arizona. Its habit is known as tabular. Such crystals are often extremely thin. Wulfenite belongs to the tetragonal crystal system.

THE GENERAL SHAPE of crystals is called their habit and is an important part of crystallography. Crystal habit is useful in identification and in well-formed crystals may be so characteristic of a particular metal that no other feature is needed to identify it. The forms (pp. 82–83) or group of forms that are developed by an individual crystal are often what give it a particular habit. As crystals grow, some faces develop more than others, and it is their relative sizes that create different shapes. Most minerals tend to occur in groups of many crystals rather than as single crystals and rarely show fine crystal shapes. These are called aggregates.

TWO FORMS
These "mushrooms" show two forms of calcite crystals: The "stems" are scalenohedrons and have eight of twelve triangular faces. The "caps" are formed by rhombohedra in parallel position. This group comes from Cumbria, England.

STALACTITIC
The black, lustrous aggregates of goethite in this group are described as stalactitic. The group comes from Koblenz, Rhineland, Germany. Goethite is of the orthorhombic crystal system. It is an important iron ore.

MASSIVE
Crystals which grow in a mass, in which individual crystals cannot be clearly seen, are described as massive. Dumortierite is a rare mineral which is usually massive like this piece from Bahia, Brazil.

ACICULAR
Looking like a sea urchin, the radiating slender mesolite crystals in this aggregate are described as acicular, meaning needle-like. They are very fragile and, like needles, can pierce your skin. This group comes from Bombay, India.

CRYSTAL-SHAPED
The Giant's Causeway near Portrush in County Antrim, Northern Ireland, looks like a collection of hexagonal crystals. However, the phenomenon is not crystal growth but jointing due to contraction as the basaltic lava cooled.

PISOLITIC
This polished slab of limestone from Czechoslovakia is described as pisolitic. Pisolites are round pea-sized aggregates of crystals built of concentric layers, in this case of calcium carbonate.

DENDRITIC
The term used to describe the habit of these copper crystals is dendritic, meaning tree-like. They come from Broken Hill, New South Wales, Australia. Copper often forms in hydrothermal deposits (pp. 94–95), filling holes in some basaltic lava flows, but is also found as grains in sandstones.

PRISMATIC
Beryl crystals are mostly found in granite pegmatites (p. 94) and can grow to be very large. Those illustrated are prismatic – they are longer in one direction than the other. They were found in 1930 in a quarry in Maine and were over 30 ft (9 m) long.

LENTICULAR
Twinned (pp. 90–91) clear crystals of gypsum form the "ears" on the mass of lenticular crystals from Winnipeg, Canada. Lenticular means shaped like a lentil or lens, from the Latin *lenticula*, a lentil.

Twinned gypsum crystal

Bladed hornblende crystal

Globular caldite crystal aggregate

CORALLOIDAL
Aggregated crystals that look like coral are said to have a coralloidal habit. This mass of pale-green aragonite crystals came from Eisenberg, Styria, Austria.

GLOBULAR
These aggregated crystals of calcite look a bit like scoops of ice cream and are described as globular, meaning spherical. The other crystals are clear quartz, and the group came from Valenciana mine, Guanajuato, Mexico.

BLADED
The prismatic black crystal in this group is a hornblende crystal and an example of a bladed crystal. The buff-colored crystals are prismatic serandite and the white crystals are analcime. The group was found at Mont-St.-Hilaire, Quebec, Canada.

QUARTZ IN A CAVE
Crystal growth is influenced by the physical and chemical conditions at the time. Many good crystals grow in cavities which can vary in size from small potato stones (pp. 76–77) to huge caves, as shown in this 19th-century impression of a quartz grotto.

Discovery – recovery

THE SEARCH FOR MINERAL deposits including metals and gemstones has been going on since prehistoric times. Some minerals, such as copper, occur in great quantity; others, such as silver, gold, and diamond, are found in much smaller quantities but fetch higher prices. If mining is to be profitable, large quantities of the mineral must occur in one area and be relatively easy to extract, either by surface quarrying, panning, or dredging, or, if necessary, by deep mining. Minerals from which useful metals such as copper, iron, and tin are extracted are called ores.

19th-century engraving of miners descending the shaft at Wieliczka salt mine, Poland

Chalcopyrite

SCATTERED GRAINS
Rocks of less than one percent ore are worked today by open-pit quarrying. The ore, such as this chalcopyrite copper ore, occurs as small grains scattered through the rock body. The whole rock has to be worked, a huge amount of gangue, or waste, is produced, and an enormous hole is left.

Copper ore

Quartz

RICH VEIN
Larger concentrations of ore occur in veins, but most high-grade ores have been found and in many cases worked out. Ores in veins are usually worked by deep mining. This vein in altered granite contains chalcopyrite and quartz.

ROMANS IN CORNWALL
The Romans knew of the rich tin deposits in Cornwall, England. Mining techniques have improved since then, but the ore still has to be crushed and separated from the gangue minerals and then refined.

Ingot of refined Cornish tin, produced in 1860

Blue crystals of liroconite, a copper arsenate, from a secondary-enriched layer

Vein of covellite, a copper sulfide, from a secondary sulfide enrichment layer

GRADUAL IMPROVEMENT
The natural process of "secondary alteration and enrichment" can improve relatively low-grade ores to higher concentrations. Groundwaters filter down through the upper layers of rock and carry elements downward. These are redeposited in lower layers which are thus enriched. Enriched layers in copper deposits may contain azurite, malachite, and sometimes liroconite, or sulfide minerals such as bornite, chalcocite, and covellite.

Panning is a simple method of separating minerals. Light gangue minerals are washed away by the swirling action of water in a metal or wood pan, leaving the wanted minerals behind. This technique is often used to sort out gem-rich river gravels in areas such as Myanmar (formerly Burma) and Thailand.

Panning for gold in the Irrawaddy River, Myanmar. The prospector looks for the glint of gold grains within the waste.

LAST TO GO

Granite pegmatites characteristically consist of large crystals and are the source of many fine gems, including tourmaline (pp. 112–113), topaz (pp. 112–113), and beryl (pp. 108–109). They are formed by the crystallization of the last fluids left after most of the granite has solidified.

Tourmaline crystal

DOWN UNDER

Much mining activity takes place underground. This is the Coober Pedy opal mine in South Australia – a source of fine white opals (pp. 110–111).

SMALLER THAN SOME

These beryl crystals measure about 8 x 6 in (20 x 14 cm) but are small compared to some crystals found in pegmatites.

ON THE SURFACE

One third of the diamonds (pp. 104–105) produced in the world each year come from the Argyle mine in Western Australia. They are mined by surface quarrying.

Growing from seed

MELTDOWN
Natural bismuth does occur, but artificial crystal groups, like this one, are often produced by melting and then cooling the metal. Bismuth is used in solders, electric fuses, and pigments.

SCIENTISTS HAVE TRIED TO MAKE CRYSTALS like those found in the earth's crust for well over a century. Natural crystals often contain impurities or are flawed in some way (pp. 90–91), but synthetic ones can be made flawless. They can also be made to grow a particular shape and size for specific needs. In recent times a range of artificial crystals has become important to modern technology. Grown crystals are built into almost every electronic or optical device made today. The need for a huge amount of perfect crystals has led to more and more synthetic crystals being made, and it could be said that future developments in electronics will depend on the development of crystal-growing techniques.

DRAWN OUT
Pure silicon does not occur naturally, so crystals are made artificially for a variety of uses (pp. 98–99). Quartz sand is heated to produce nearly pure silicon. In one process a seed crystal on the end of a rotating rod is dipped into the melt and slowly removed; this is known as "drawing a crystal."

IN A FLUX
Many emeralds are produced by the flux-fusion technique. A powder made of the components of emerald is heated in a crucible with a solid known as a flux. The flux melts, the powder dissolves, and the mixture is left to cool and form crystals. This method is extremely slow. It takes several months for a crystal to grow.

Cut synthetic emerald

Synthetic emerald crystal

VOYAGE OF DISCOVERY
Crystal growing is important enough for experiments to be done in space. Here, astronaut George Nelson is photographing a protein-crystal-growth experiment on board the space shuttle *Discovery* in 1988.

Melt technique

Excellent crystals may be grown by slow cooling or evaporation of a supersaturated solution (no more will dissolve) of a salt such as halite, alum, or ammonium dihydrogen phosphate (ADP). In the experiment shown, powdered ADP containing a small chrome-alum impurity has been completely dissolved in boiling water and then cooled.

The liquid cools rapidly. Stubby, cloudy, prismatic (p. 92) crystals form.

The crystals grow more slowly, allowing them to become clearer.

At room temperature, crystals still grow slowly due to evaporation.

Cooling stops, but evaporation continues. The crystals slowly grow.

FIRE BOULES

The flame-fusion technique was perfected by French mineral expert A. Verneuil in about 1900. It is used to make spinel (pp. 116–117), rutile (pp.70–71), and corundum (pp. 106–107). Powdered material is fed through a flame to fuse into liquid drops which drip onto a support. By gradually pulling the support from the heat, a single crystal, or boule, is formed.

HENRI MOISSAN (1852-1907)
French chemist Henri Moissan tried to produce artificial diamonds in iron crucibles at the Edison workshops in Paris.

EUREKA!
In 1970, the General Electric Company announced the laboratory creation of gem-quality diamonds, two of which are shown here.

Support for growing crystal

Synthetic sapphire boule

Synthetic rubies produced in a crucible

Two halves of synthetic ruby boule

GROWN IN SIZE
The French chemist Frémy was the first to grow gem-quality crystals of a reasonable size, in 1877. He discovered a method of making rubies by melting the necessary materials together and fusing them in a porcelain crucible at very high temperatures.

1890 crucible containing a mass of small gemstones

ABRASIVE CHARACTER
The artificial material carborundum (silicon carbide) is produced by the fusion of coke and sand heated in electrically fired furnaces. It is nearly as hard as diamond – 9.5 on Mohs' hardness scale (pp. 88–89) – and is therefore mostly used as an abrasive.

Hexagonal carborundum crystal

GOLD FEVER
Over the centuries many people have tried to find a way to change nonprecious metals into gold. A complicated process if this detail of *The Alchemist at Work* by David Teniers the Elder (1582-1649) is anything to go by.

Crystals at work

CRYSTALS PLAY AN IMPORTANT PART in this age of rapid technological and social change. Although the basic understanding of crystals was developed before the 20th century, it is only during the last part of this century that crystal technology has become so important. Crystals are now used in control circuits, machines, electronics, medicine, industrial tools, and communications. We even sometimes use crystals when shopping – in credit cards. From the crystal laboratory (pp. 96–97) have come silicon chips, ruby laser rods, and many forms of diamonds for tools.

DIAMOND WINDOW
The properties of diamond have led to it being used in space where it has to withstand extreme conditions. Diamond was used in this window for an infrared radiometer experiment on the Pioneer Venus probe. It had to withstand a temperature of 840°F (250°C) near the surface of the planet Venus.

Silicon wafer

SILICON SLICE
Silicon chips are made from very thin slices called wafers cut from artificial crystals of pure silicon (pp. 96–97). The wafers are etched with electronic circuits, one for each chip. The circuit patterns are transferred on to a wafer from a piece of film called a matrix.

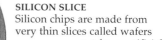

Silicon chip matrix

Silicon chip in protective covering

CIRCUIT BOARD
Many different chips are needed in a large computer. Each chip has a different circuit and runs a different part of the computer. The chips are protected in individual cases then connected to the others on a circuit board.

SMART CARDS
There is a tiny built-in mini-computer on a silicon chip in each of these "smart cards." Smart cards are still being developed but some are already in limited use. It is expected that in the near future people will be able to use them to store and update personal information, such as the state of their bank account, as well as to make payments.

RUBY ROD
Synthetic ruby crystals are used in some lasers. The heated atoms in the ruby are stimulated by light of a certain wavelength (p. 85) and emit radiation waves in step with the stimulating light. This makes a beam of pure red laser light.

Location of silicon chip

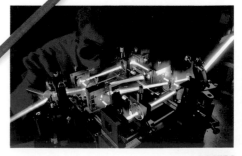

LASERS
This scientist is experimenting with laser beams. Laser beams can be focused to very small points, generating intense heat. This is put to use in welding, drilling, and surgery.

Diamond tools

Diamonds are used in a vast number of jobs mainly because they are so hard. They are used in sawing, drilling, grinding, and polishing – from quarrying stone to performing delicate eye surgery – and come in a large range of sizes, shapes, and strengths. Natural and synthetic diamonds are used, but more than 80 percent of industrial diamonds are synthetic.

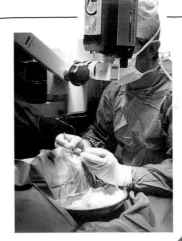

A surgeon using a diamond-bladed scalpel in delicate eye surgery

DRILL BITS

Diamond-tipped drills are used for drilling all types of rock. They are used for drilling oil wells and in prospecting for metals and minerals. Some bits contain diamonds set in the surface. The diamonds are different shapes for different purposes. Other bits are covered with tiny pieces of diamond grit, or abrasive.

Drill bit containing surface-set natural diamonds

Drill bit covered with synthetic diamond abrasive

DIAMOND SCALPEL

As well as being hard, diamond does not corrode. This property is one reason why diamonds are used in surgery. This surgical scalpel contains a blade made from a natural diamond.

Diamond blade

DIAMOND GRIT

Grit and powders are made from synthetic diamonds or poor-quality natural stones. They are used for polishing and grinding.

DIAMOND WIRE

Cutting with a diamond wire keeps the loss of material to a minimum. Wires can be used for cutting blocks of stone from quarries as well as for controlled demolition of concrete buildings. The wire can be used around a drum or as a continuous loop.

"Bead" containing synthetic diamond abrasive

Cutting segment containing synthetic diamond abrasive

SAW BLADE

Saws set with diamonds are used for cutting glass, ceramics, and rocks. The blades have a rim of industrial diamonds in a "carrier" such as brass. This rim is bonded to a steel disk. As the blade cuts, the carrier wears away rapidly and exposes new diamonds.

Cutting an opening for a window in brickwork using a diamond saw

Good vibrations

QUARTZ IS ONE OF THE MOST COMMON MINERALS in the earth's crust. It is widely distributed as veins (pp. 94–95) and is associated with major mineral deposits. It is one of the chief materials in granite and is also the main component of sand and sandstone. As quartzite and sandstone, it is used extensively for building and in the manufacture of glass and ceramics. One of the most interesting properties of quartz crystals is piezoelectricity. This can be used to measure pressure, and quartz crystal oscillators provide fixed, very stable frequency control in radios and televisions (an oscillator is something that vibrates). The piezoelectric effect of crystals is used in gas igniters. When a crystal is "squeezed," an electric charge is produced as a spark which lights the gas. Because it so often forms perfect crystals, quartz is also used in crystal healing.

PAST FAVORITE
Quartz crystals from Brazil were important material for electronics before synthetic crystals were grown. Large quartz crystals are still found there, as demonstrated by this local miner, or *garimpeiro*.

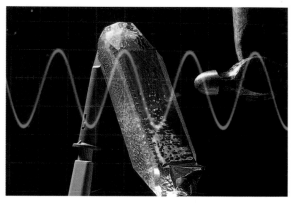

WAVES OF ENERGY
Quartz crystals are used in electronics. They can change a mechanical force, such as a blow from a hammer, into electrical energy, shown here as a wave-form on an oscilloscope screen.

Mica

Feldspar

Quartz

CRYSTAL TRIO
Large crystals of quartz can be seen in this granite pegmatite crystal group (pp. 94–95). Fine crystals of the other two major components of granite rocks, feldspar and mica, are also here.

Gold deposit

Quartz vein

GOING FOR GOLD
Many quartz veins carry metallic mineral deposits (pp. 94–95). This specimen contains gold. It came from St. David's mine, Gwynedd, Wales, an area famous for the extraction of British gold. The quartz and gold were both deposited by hydrothermal (hot, watery) fluids. In mining practice, the quartz would be considered a "gangue," or unwanted mineral.

ENGLISH PRISM
Quartz commonly crystallizes as 6-sided prisms with rhombohedral termination (pp. 82–83). The prism axis shows only 3-fold symmetry. On many crystals, alternate faces show different growth patterns. This crystal group comes from Cornwall, England.

Hexagonal, prismatic crystal

Arrangement of small faces shows left-handedness

Right-handed quartz crystal

AMBIDEXTROUS
In a quartz crystal, silicon and oxygen atoms are joined in the shape of a tetrahedron (a four-sided triangular pyramid). These tetrahedra are connected in a spiral arrangement, like a spiral staircase, and can be left- or right-handed. It is this structure which accounts for the piezoelectricity of quartz.

Left-handed quartz crystal

ALPINE ARCHITECTURE
This "twisted" group of smoky quartz crystals shows some beautiful crystal "architecture." Such crystal groups are often found in the Alps, in Europe.

Crystal pendant thought by some to help with healing

Crystal healing

The laying on of stones is an ancient art. It is thought that as light reflects off the crystals and stones, the electromagnetic field of the body – the aura – absorbs energy. The receiver can then become aware of mental and emotional causes of physical disease, and heal.

CRYSTAL CLEAR
Rock crystals from groups such as this one from Arkansas are highly prized for their beauty and clarity and are therefore often used for crystal healing.

HEALING POWER
Katrina Raphaell, shown here performing a crystal healing, is the founder of the Crystal Academy in Taos, New Mexico. She has placed stones and crystals upon vital nerve points of the body.

Piezoelectricity

Piezoelectricity was discovered by the brothers Pierre and Jacques Curie in 1880. They discovered that pressure on a quartz crystal causes positive and negative charges to be produced across the crystal. It was later found that an alternating electrical charge placed on a piezoelectric crystal could cause the crystal to vibrate. This is the basis of the use of quartz as oscillator plates to control radio waves and keep time.

Jacques and Pierre Curie with their parents

PURE NECESSITY
To meet the demand for pure, flawless quartz crystals necessary for making oscillator plates, synthetic crystals like this one are now grown by a hydrothermal process (pp. 96–97).

WATCH PIECE
This microthin quartz crystal slice is used to keep time in a quartz watch. The photograph is greatly enlarged.

Quartz crystal slice

SPLIT-SECOND TIMING
The crystal slice in a quartz watch vibrates more than 30,000 times each second. It is this regularity of vibration which makes it a good timekeeper.

Quartz

Q UARTZ IS SILICON DIOXIDE. It occurs as individual crystals and fine-grained masses in a large variety of forms, patterns, and colors. If conditions are right, giant crystals can grow (Brazil is famous for these). The largest recorded rock crystal was about 20 ft (6 m) long and weighed more than 48 tons (44,000 kg). Other sources of fine quartz include the Swiss Alps, the USA, and Madagascar. Quartz is tough and has no cleavage (p. 85), making it ideal for carving and cutting, and it is very popular as a gemstone. The name quartz usually refers to individual crystals or coarse-grained aggregates while the fine-grained materials are called chalcedonies or jaspers.

QUARTZ CRYSTAL
Crystal system: trigonal; hardness: 7; specific gravity: 2.65.

DUNES AND DUST
As quartz is relatively hard and common, it forms the major part of sand and also of dust in the air. Dust can therefore damage gems of 6 or less on Mohs' hardness scale (pp. 88–89).

Single crystals

The best-known single crystals of quartz are colorless rock crystal, purple amethyst, rose quartz, smoky quartz, and yellow citrine. These transparent crystals often occur in large enough pieces to be cut as gemstones.

BACCHUS BY CARAVAGGIO
A 16th-century French verse tells how Bacchus, the god of wine, declares in a rage that the first person he passes will be eaten by tigers. This turns out to be a beautiful maiden called Amethyst. The goddess Diana quickly turns Amethyst into a white stone to save her from the tigers. Regretting his anger, Bacchus pours red wine over the stone as an offering to Diana, so turning the stone purple.

AMETHYST
The most highly prized form of quartz is amethyst. The best comes from two kinds of source. In the Ural Mountains in the USSR crystals occur in veins in granite. In Brazil, Uruguay, and India crystals of superb color are often found in cavities in basalt.

ROSE QUARTZ
Single rose quartz crystals are very rare and most rose quartz is massive. It is best cut as cabochons (pp. 114–115) or used for carvings and beads. Some material can be polished to display a star.

Amethyst

Garnet

Agate

Pearl

Aquamarine

Agate

Amazonite

RARE BEAUTY
This 19th-century gold box is set with a superb rare citrine surrounded by a garnet (p. 114), an amazonite, two pearls (p. 123), two aquamarines (p. 109), three agates, and three amethysts.

IMPURE OF HEART
Colorless rock crystal is the purest form of quartz, the many other colors being caused by impurities. Amethyst and citrine contain iron, rose quartz contains titanium and iron, and smoky quartz contains aluminum.

Massive

There are several massive varieties of quartz which are composed of very tiny grains or fibers. Chalcedony – such as carnelian, chrysoprase, and agate – and jasper are distinguished by the different arrangements of these grains. Tiger's-eye and hawk's-eye form when tiny fibers of asbestos are replaced by quartz and iron oxides.

AGATE
The quartz grains in chalcedony are arranged in layers and their buildup is clearly visible in the different colored layers of agate. In this specimen they crystallized progressively toward the middle of a cavity in lava.

Entry point for quartz solution into lava cavity

Bands of agate

TIGER'S-EYE
Originally this vein of tiger's-eye contained silky blue crystals of asbestos. These were dissolved by solutions which deposited quartz and iron oxides in their place. The structure of the tiny fibers of asbestos was exactly reproduced by the quartz, and this gives rise to the light reflection or the "cat's-eye."

Polished tiger's-eye showing the cat's-eye effect called chatoyancy

A tiger shows why tiger's-eye is so named

Vein of carnelian

Rock crystal

CARNELIAN
Carnelian is the name given to translucent (pp. 86–87) orange-red chalcedony. Most specimens are the result of heat-treating a less attractive chalcedony. The treatment turns iron-bearing minerals into iron oxides which give the more desirable orange-red colors.

JASPER
The interlocking quartz crystals in jasper are arranged in a random mass. They are mixed with colorful impurities, making the stone opaque.

CHRYSOPRASE
At its finest, chrysoprase is a vibrant green and the most valuable of the chalcedonies. It has been used in ornament and decorative patterns since prehistoric times. A recent source of some of the best material is Queensland, Australia.

Chrysoprase cameo set in gold

Diamond

DIAMOND CRYSTAL
Crystal system: cubic; hardness: 10; specific gravity: 3.5.

THE WORD DIAMOND is derived from the Greek word *adamas*, meaning "unconquerable," given to the stone because of its supreme hardness. Diamond is made of pure carbon and has an immensely strong crystal structure (pp. 84–85). It is this which makes it the hardest of all minerals. Evidence suggests that diamonds were formed up to 125 miles (200 km) deep within the earth, and some stones may be as much as three billion years old. Diamonds were first discovered over 2,000 years ago and came mainly from river gravel in India. In 1725, they were found in Brazil, which remained the major source until production in South Africa became significant in 1870. Today, about 20 countries produce diamonds. The top producer is Australia, which supplies a quarter of the world's needs, mainly for industrial purposes (pp. 98–99). Diamond has great luster and fire, properties which are best revealed in the brilliant cut (pp. 74–75).

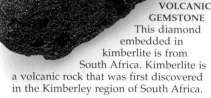

Diamond

VOLCANIC GEMSTONE
This diamond embedded in kimberlite is from South Africa. Kimberlite is a volcanic rock that was first discovered in the Kimberley region of South Africa.

ROUGH DIAMONDS
Rough diamonds mined from kimberlites often have lustrous crystal faces; alluvial diamonds – those recovered from gravel – can be dull. This is because they may have been carried long distances in rough water with other rocks and gravel.

Mined diamonds

Alluvial diamonds

Diamonds

DIAMOND RUSH
In 1925 some very rich alluvial deposits were discovered at Lichtenburg, South Africa. The government decided to allocate claims (areas of land to mine) on the outcome of a race. So, on August 20, 1926, 10,000 miners lined up and had to race about 218 yards (200 m) to stake their claims.

SPOT THE DIAMONDS
Diamond-bearing gravel is the result of one of nature's sorting processes. Seriously flawed or fractured stones are more likely to be broken up and eroded away, so a high proportion of the diamonds found in gravel are of gem quality.

UNCONQUERABLE BELIEF
Napoleon Bonaparte is depicted here as First Consul wearing a sword set with the Regent diamond. He hoped the diamond would bring him victory in battle; according to an ancient belief, a diamond made its wearer unconquerable.

RICH MIX
Conglomerate rock is a mixture of different sizes of rounded pebbles and mineral grains which have been deposited from water and cemented together. This specimen from the west coast of South Africa is particularly rich in diamonds.

INDIAN DIAMOND
This rough diamond is embedded in a sandy conglomerate found near Hyderabad in India. This area was the source of many famous large diamonds such as the Koh-i-noor and the Regent.

VALLEY OF DIAMONDS
Sindbad was once stranded in the legendary Valley of Diamonds. On the valley floor were diamonds guarded by snakes. Sindbad escaped by tying himself to meat thrown down by a diamond collector. As intended by the collector, a bird carried the meat out of the valley stuck with diamonds – and Sindbad!

BUTTERFLY BROOCH
This butterfly brooch is set with over 150 diamonds.

MURCHISON SNUFFBOX
This gold box set with diamonds bears a portrait of Czar Alexander II of Russia. It was presented in 1867 by the czar to Sir Roderick Murchison, the second director of the British Geological Survey, in recognition of Sir Roderick's geological work in Russia.

A GIRL'S BEST FRIEND
"Diamonds Are a Girl's Best Friend" is the title of a song from the film *Gentlemen Prefer Blondes*. Marilyn Monroe starred in the film wearing a yellow diamond called the Moon of Baroda.

BRILLIANT COLORS
Most natural diamonds are near-colorless; truly colorless ones are rare. A few stones are also found of all colors in the spectrum (pp. 86–87) and good-quality ones are known as fancies.

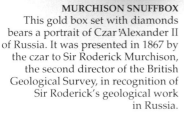

AGNÈS SOREL (c 1422-1450)
Agnès Sorel, the mistress of the French king Charles VII, was the first commoner in France to break the law made by Louis IX in the 13th century decreeing that only kings and nobles could wear diamonds.

Famous diamonds

Diamonds of exceptional beauty and rarity are highly prized. Some have long, recorded histories and others have inspired fantastic legends. Most belong to the rich and famous.

THE JEWEL IN THE CROWN
The Koh-i-noor (mountain of light) is claimed to be the oldest large diamond. It was probably found in India and after belonging to Mogul kings was presented to Queen Victoria in 1850. Its cut, shown in this replica, was unimpressive, so it was recut. Today, it is in the British crown jewels.

PREMIER DIAMOND
In 1905 the Cullinan crystal was found in the Premier diamond mine in the Transvaal, South Africa. It weighed 3,106 carats and is still the largest diamond ever found. This replica shows its actual size. In 1908 it was cut into 9 large and 96 lesser stones. The two largest, Cullinan I and II, are in the British crown jewels (pp. 116–117).

BLUE HOPE
The Hope has a reputation for bringing bad luck, but the sinister stories are untrue. It is 45.52 carats and is now in the Smithsonian Institution, Washington D.C.

Corundum

RUBY AND SAPPHIRE are varieties of the mineral corundum, an aluminum oxide. Only true red stones are called rubies, and the term *sapphire* on its own indicates a blue stone. Other colors are described as sapphire, that is, yellow sapphire and pink sapphire. Corundum is next to diamond in hardness, so gem crystals are resistant to wear. It is pleochroic, which means the color of a stone varies when it is viewed in different directions. Most gem crystals are recovered from gravel, and the most famous sources are Myanmar (formerly Burma), Kashmir, and Sri Lanka. Today, Australia is the largest producer of blue and golden sapphires. Other producers include Thailand and countries in East Africa.

CORUNDUM
Crystal system: trigonal; hardness: 9; specific gravity: 3.96–4.05.

Twin sapphire crystals

KASHMIR BLUE
Kashmir has a reputation for producing sapphires of the finest blue, like these two examples. The term *Kashmir blue* is often used to describe sapphires of this color from other parts of the world.

Sapphire intergrown with tourmaline

SOURCE REVEALED
A famous source of fine sapphires is in a valley in the Kanskar range of the Himalayas in Kashmir. It is said the source was only revealed after a landslide in about 1881.

MYANMAR CRYSTAL
Most of the highest-quality rubies come from the Mogok region in Myanmar, and this fine crystal embedded in calcite is a good example. Rubies from Myanmar, Pakistan, and Afghanistan are often found in calcite.

RUSKIN'S RUBY
This Myanmar ruby crystal was presented to the Natural History Museum in London by the philosopher John Ruskin in December 1887. It is about 162 carats. Its deep red color is the most admired color for a ruby and is sometimes described as "pigeon's blood" red.

Flattened prism of fine-quality ruby from the Mogok district of upper Myanmar

BAZAAR DEALING
This 1930 photograph shows ruby dealers in a Mogok bazaar. Gem-quality corundum is rare, and ruby is the most valuable variety of all. Good quality stones can fetch even higher prices than diamonds of the same size.

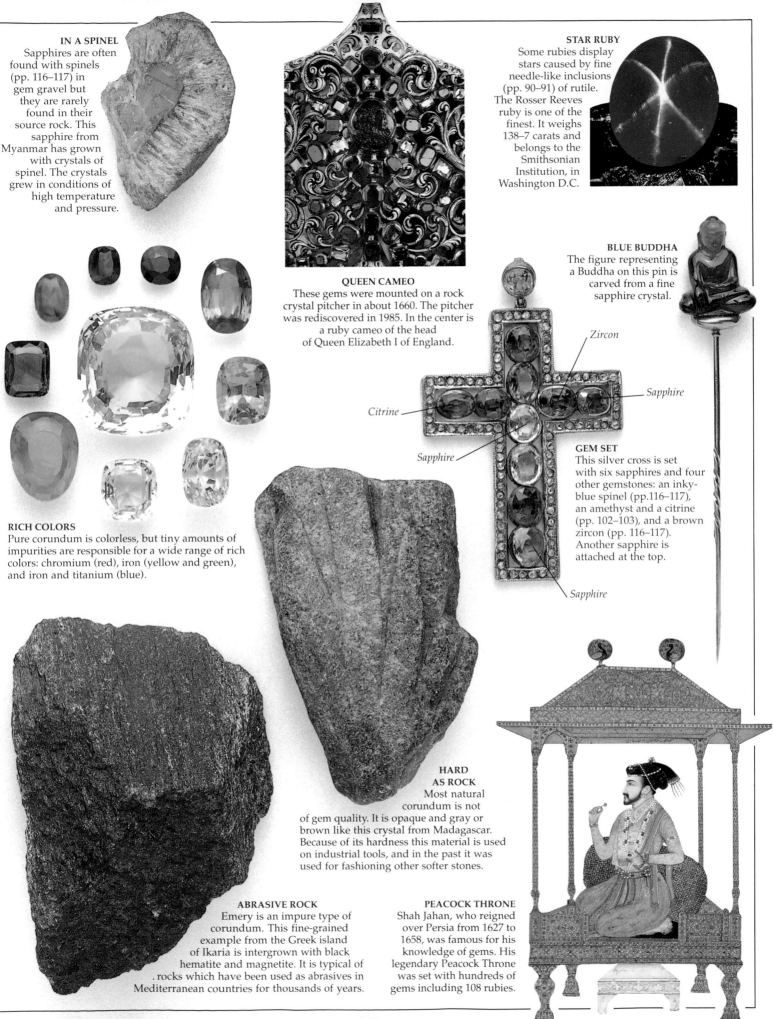

IN A SPINEL
Sapphires are often found with spinels (pp. 116–117) in gem gravel but they are rarely found in their source rock. This sapphire from Myanmar has grown with crystals of spinel. The crystals grew in conditions of high temperature and pressure.

STAR RUBY
Some rubies display stars caused by fine needle-like inclusions (pp. 90–91) of rutile. The Rosser Reeves ruby is one of the finest. It weighs 138–7 carats and belongs to the Smithsonian Institution, in Washington D.C.

QUEEN CAMEO
These gems were mounted on a rock crystal pitcher in about 1660. The pitcher was rediscovered in 1985. In the center is a ruby cameo of the head of Queen Elizabeth I of England.

BLUE BUDDHA
The figure representing a Buddha on this pin is carved from a fine sapphire crystal.

Zircon

Citrine

Sapphire

Sapphire

Sapphire

GEM SET
This silver cross is set with six sapphires and four other gemstones: an inky-blue spinel (pp.116–117), an amethyst and a citrine (pp. 102–103), and a brown zircon (pp. 116–117). Another sapphire is attached at the top.

RICH COLORS
Pure corundum is colorless, but tiny amounts of impurities are responsible for a wide range of rich colors: chromium (red), iron (yellow and green), and iron and titanium (blue).

HARD AS ROCK
Most natural corundum is not of gem quality. It is opaque and gray or brown like this crystal from Madagascar. Because of its hardness this material is used on industrial tools, and in the past it was used for fashioning other softer stones.

ABRASIVE ROCK
Emery is an impure type of corundum. This fine-grained example from the Greek island of Ikaria is intergrown with black hematite and magnetite. It is typical of rocks which have been used as abrasives in Mediterranean countries for thousands of years.

PEACOCK THRONE
Shah Jahan, who reigned over Persia from 1627 to 1658, was famous for his knowledge of gems. His legendary Peacock Throne was set with hundreds of gems including 108 rubies.

Beryl

BERYLS ARE POPULAR AS GEMS because of their fine colors and resistance to wear. The most well-known varieties are emerald (green) and aquamarine (blue-green). Yellow beryl is known as heliodor, and pink beryl is morganite. The name beryl can be traced to Greek, Roman, and possibly Sanskrit sources, and it is highly likely that aquamarine and helidor were known in prehistoric times. Beryl is found in pegmatites (pp. 94–95) and granites and in its massive, opaque, non-gem form can occur in crystals weighing many tons. The recordholder is a crystal which was found in Madagascar weighing 36 tons and measuring about 60 ft (18 m) long.

BERYL CRYSTAL
Crystal system: hexagonal; hardness: 7.5; specific gravity 2.63–2.91.

SOVIET HOST
A typical source of emeralds is mica schist. This kind of source was found in the early 1800s in the Ural Mountains, Russia. Many of these crystals have mica and amphibloe inclusions (pp. 90–91), the same rock as the host.

SPANISH SPOILS
The Chibcha Indians of Colombia mined emeralds which, through trade, reached the Incas of Peru and the Aztecs of Mexico. They were seen there in the early 1500s by the Spanish, who determined to find their source. They did not find the Chivor mine until 1537, and most of the emeralds sent back to the Spanish court were pillaged from the Incas' treasure.

MINED FOR LIFE
The finest emeralds in the world come from around Muzo and Chivor in Colombia. Many are mined and exported illegally, and there are often robberies and murders.

An 1870 engraving showing convicts working the Colombian emerald mines

ANCIENT ACCESS
Emeralds were mined near the Red Sea in Egypt from about 1500 B.C. The mines were rediscovered in 1816 by the French adventurer Cailliaud, but attempts at mining were not a success. This old entrance to one of Cleopatra's mines was discovered in about 1900.

FINE CUT
This exceptionally fine, 911-carat, cut aquamarine belongs to the Smithsonian Institution in Washington, D.C.

SECOND-CLASS CRYSTAL
A few emeralds are still found in Egypt. They come from an area of granite, schist, and serpentine. Most crystals are blue-green with many inclusions and do not compare in quality with the best Colombian emeralds.

COLOR CAUSES
Pure beryl is colorless. The spectacular reds and pinks are caused by manganese, the blues and yellows by iron. The beautiful emerald green is due to tiny amounts of chromium or vanadium.

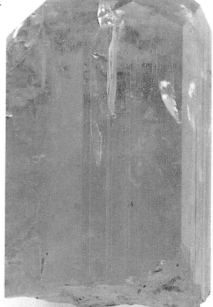

SEA-GREEN
Aquamarine means "sea water," which accurately describes its color. It has a range from pale green to blue, caused by varying amounts of different forms of iron. It is relatively common, with sources in many countries; the main source is Brazil.

DRY RED
Red beryl is extremely rare and is the only natural beryl that contains no water in its crystal structure. It occurs in "dry" volcanic rocks in the western USA. This fine specimen comes from the Wah Wah Mountains in Utah.

Morganite

Heliodor

Tourmaline inclusions

TURKISH DELIGHT
The Topkapi Palace Treasury in Istanbul, Turkey, contains many pieces with fine emeralds. The hilt of this 18th-century dagger holds three, plus one cut as a hexagonal slice and hinged over a small watch at the end.

GEM BELTS
This large crystal of beryl is made up of zones of the varieties morganite and heliodor. This gem-quality specimen comes from Brazil, but other sources of these varieties include California, Madagascar, and Pakistan.

Opal

OPAL
Crystal system: amorphous or poorly crystalline; hardness: 5.5–6.5; specific gravity: 1.98–2.25.

T<small>HE</small> POPULARITY OF OPAL has risen and fallen over the centuries. The ancient Romans used it as a symbol of power but since then, at different times, it has been considered to be unlucky. The Aztecs mined opal over 500 years ago in Central America; this area is still an important source, especially of fire opal, from Mexico. Australia is the top producer of both black and white opals; they were first discovered there in the 1870s. Opal is one of the few noncrystalline gems. It has a tendency to crack and chip, especially under extreme temperature changes or after a hard knock. The exciting flashes of color shown by precious opal are best displayed in cabochons, but Mexican fire opals are usually cut as brilliant or step cuts (pp. 74–75).

ROMAN SOURCE
This piece of white opal comes from Cervenica, Czechoslovakia, the source used by the Romans. This region was once part of Hungary, and the opal from here is usually described as Hungarian.

THE PLAGUE OF VENICE
This detail of a painting by Antonio Zanchi depicts the Black Death of the 14th century. The people in Venice, Italy, noticed that opals became brilliant when a wearer caught the disease and dulled when the person died. This reinforced the belief that opals were unlucky.

FLASH OF LIGHTNING
The finest black opal comes from Lightning Ridge, New South Wales, Australia. Against its dark body the color flashes are quite dramatic and this attraction, coupled with its greater rarity, make it more valuable than white opal.

NONFLASHY
Nonprecious opal without flashes of color is called potch opal. Rose opal is potch, but its striking color has led to its being used in beads and decorative jewelry. This specimen comes from France; there are other sources in Idaho.

AUSTRALIAN FAIR
All the major Australian opal deposits occur in sedimentary rocks in the Great Artesian Basin. Famous mines include White Cliffs, Lightning Ridge, and Coober Pedy. A popular way of marketing the opal is in doublets and triplets (layers of gem and colored glass fused together).

GLASSY LOOK
Clear, glassy-looking opal (hyalite) occurs in cavities in volcanic lavas. This example is from Bohemia (Czechoslovakia) but there are several other sources. If similar material shows a play of color, it is known as water opal. Another kind of opal, called hydrophane, is opaque but appears colorless in water.

Greatly enlarged photograph of precious opal, showing the ordered silica spheres in the structure that cause the play of colors

FLASHING LIGHTS
Precious opal displays flashes of different colors. The colors depend on the size of the silica spheres in the structure. Opal with a background color of gray, blue, or black is called black. Others are called white.

ON THE MAP
"Prospector's brooches," shaped like the map of Australia, were made to mark the arrival on the gemstone market of Australian opal. This one is thought to have been made around 1875.

Opal cameo *Dawn with Cupid and Psyche* now in the Natural History Museum, London

MEXICAN FIRE
Mexico has long been famous for its fire opal. This is a nearly transparent variety, still showing flashes of color. It ranges from yellow to orange and red.

MOVED IN
The opal localities in Australia are extremely hot, so when mines are exhausted, those excavations near the surface are adapted to provide relatively cool and pleasant living conditions.

PRECIOUS FOSSIL
Opal often replaces the tissues of wood, and bones and shells of ancient animals, in a kind of fossilization. It grows bit by bit in place of the original material. This piece of wood from Nevada has been replaced by precious and potch opal.

BEAUTIFUL BOULDER
Boulder opal is hardened sandy clay with variable amounts of iron oxides and layers of precious opal. If enough iron is present, the rock is very dark brown and flat surfaces of opal can be carved into beautiful cameos.

Precious opal   *Potch opal*

OPAL FRUIT
This was an aggregate (pp. 92–93) of radiating crystals of glauberite. It has been completely replaced by precious opal. This kind of opal is found in Australia and is popularity known as pineapple opal.

DRUNK AND DRIVING
Opal was given a bad name in the 17th-century court of the French king Louis XIV. He named his coaches after gemstones. The driver of the *Opal* was usually drunk, and the coach was considered unlucky! This is a detail of a picture by Van der Meulen called *Entry into Arras by Louis XIV and Marie Thérèse.*

Other gemstones

THE PROPERTIES OF A GEMSTONE are said to be beauty, rarity, and durability, and these standards have been applied to many species. As well as quartz (pp. 102–103), diamond (pp. 104–105), ruby and sapphire (pp. 106–107), beryl (pp. 108–109), and opal (pp. 110–111), gemstones to be seen in jewelers' shops include topaz, tourmaline, garnet, peridot, and many others. Some species, such as kunzite, sphene, and fluorite, are too soft or rare to be in general circulation as gemstones and are cut only for collectors on the basis of their beauty and rarity.

MARVELOUS GEMS
"Fishing for pearls and gathering turquoises" from *The Book of Marvels* by Marco Polo.

Topaz

The mineral we know as topaz was only given the name in the first half of the 18th century. Prior to that its history is not clear. The name topaz is said to come from *Topazius*, the Greek name for Zabargad, an island in the Red Sea. This island is, however, a source of what we now call peridot (pp. 114–115).

TOPAZ CRYSTAL
Crystal system: orthorhombic; hardness: 8; specific gravity: 3.52–3.56.

CRYSTAL FAME
The most famous source of topaz is Brazil, which is where this pale-blue crystal comes from. It is also found in Mexico, USA, Sri Lanka, Japan, USSR, Nigeria, and Zaire.

Line of cleavage

NEEDS PROTECTION
Although it is very hard, topaz can be broken easily because it has one direction of perfect cleavage (pp. 84–85). A line of cleavage can be seen clearly in this crystal. If the topaz is used in jewelry, the setting must therefore provide protection from accidental knocks.

ONE OF THE BEST
The finest golden topaz crystals come from the Ouro Preto area in Brazil, and this wedge-shaped prism is typical of them. Some may show color zoning from golden brown to pink. Gems containing a hint of pink are often called imperial topaz.

TOPAZ TRICKS
Like diamond, topaz is commonly found in gravel as rounded, waterworn pebbles. It also has a specific gravity very similar to that of diamond and this has led to some premature celebrations.

WATER COLORS
Topaz is an aluminum silicate containing about 20 percent water and fluorine. Those crystals with more water than fluorine are golden brown or, rarely, pink; those with more fluorine than water are blue or colorless.

BRAZILIAN PRINCESS
This topaz was cut in 1977 and weighed 21,327 carats. The largest cut stone today is 36,853 carats.

Tourmaline

Tourmaline is a mineral with a complex chemistry. It crystallizes as prisms with flat or wedge-shaped terminations. Every crystal has a different structure at each end, sometimes indicated by different colors. This gives tourmaline an unusual electrical property. If a crystal is gently warmed, one end becomes positively charged and the other negatively charged, which is the reason for its tendency to attract dust.

TOURMALINE CRYSTAL
Crystal system: trigonal; hardness: 7–7.5; specific gravity: 3–3.25.

MEDICINE OR MINERAL
Philosopher John Ruskin, shown here in 1885, wrote "the chemistry of tourmaline is more like a medieval doctor's prescription than the making of a respectable mineral!"

FRAMED UP
This slice across a tourmaline prism shows typical three-fold symmetry and a triangular cross-section. The zones of color illustrate how the crystal was built up in layers, each layer being a different phase of crystallization. The final shape of the crystal is controlled by the last phase, which in this case formed a hexagonal "frame."

The growth rings seen in some crystals are similar to those of tree trunks

BLACK AND GREEN
Tourmaline is pleochroic, which means it is a different color when viewed down different axes (pp. 82–83). These green crystals would be almost black if viewed down the long axis.

Tourmaline crystal

CLOSE NEIGHBORS
This tourmaline is unusual in being attached to its neighbor (quartz) by a prism face. The pink prism crystallized first, then green tourmaline formed the terminations.

SET IN GRANITE
Gem quality tourmalines are most often found in pegmatite veins (pp. 94–95) or granites. Brazil, USSR, USA, East Africa, and Afghanistan have all produced fine crystals.

Cut stone showing the two colors of watermelon tourmaline

MULTICOLORED
Tourmaline shows the greatest color range of any gemstone, and some crystals are themselves more than one color. Watermelon tourmaline has pink cores and green outer zones.

Tourmaline crystal

Continued on next page

GARNET CRYSTALS
Crystal system: cubic;
hardness: 6.5–7.5;
specific gravity:
3.52–4.32.

Ring set with
almandine garnet

Cut demantoid
garnet

DEMANTOID
Emerald-green
demantoid is the
most prized of all
the garnets. The
finest stones come
from the Ural
Mountains in
the USSR.

Garnet

Garnet is the name of a family of chemically related minerals that includes almandine, pyrope, spessartine, grossular, and andradite. They can all be found as gemstones, the almandine-pyrope group being the most widely used. Because of the different chemical compositions, garnet occurs in most colors other than blue. Sources of gem-quality material include Czechoslovakia, South Africa, USA, Australia, Brazil, and Sri Lanka.

Cut
pyrope
garnet

PYROPE
The deep-red garnet, pyrope, was
popular in the 19th century. Most stones
came from Bohemia.

Spessartine
cabochon

SPESSARTINE
The beautiful orange colors of spessartine are
caused by manganese. Spessartine is not often
seen in jewelry, as gem-quality crystals are rare.

FRUITY NAME
"Garnet" may come from *pomum granatum*, Latin for
pomegranate. The gem color of the almandine-
pyrope group is similar to that of the pomegranate.

ALMANDINE
Garnet commonly crystallizes
as icositetrahedrons, like these
almandine crystals. Almandine
usually has a very deep color
so it is often cut as cabochons
(pp. 74–75) with the backs
hollowed out to make
it more transparent.

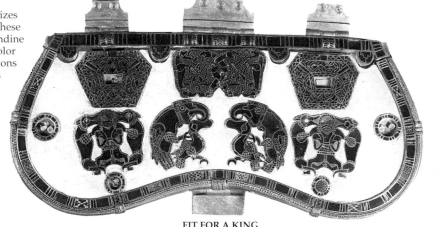

FIT FOR A KING
This fine 7th-century purse lid was among many garnet-set pieces found
in an Anglo-Saxon royal burial ship in Sutton Hoo, Suffolk, England.
The quality of the workmanship of all the pieces indicates the high
status of their owner.

ANDRADITE
Most andradite
garnet does not
occur as gem-quality
crystals. Only green
demantoid, the yellow
variety topazolite, and this
black variety, melanite, are used
as gemstones. Black garnet was
once used as mourning jewelry.

Cut grossular garnets

COLOR TRACES
Brilliant-green grossular contains trace
amounts of vanadium, while the
yellow and red stones contain iron. The
red variety is known as hessonite.

GROSSULAR
Some grossular
garnet is said to look
like gooseberries and
the name grossular
probably comes from
the Latin for gooseberry –
grossularia. This specimen
of pink grossular from Mexico
clearly shows dodecahedral crystals,
one of the two major habits of garnet.

Peridot

Peridot is a French word and may derive from the Arabic *faridat*, meaning a gem. It is the gem variety of the mineral olivine, a magnesium and iron silicate that is common in volcanic rocks.

PERIDOT CRYSTAL
Crystal system: orthorhombic; hardness: 6.5; specific gravity: 3.22–3.40.

Olivine-rich rock

Lava

Cut peridot from Arizona

Cut peridot from Norway

Cut peridot from Myanmar

Ring set with peridot

PERIDOT SUPPLIERS
The largest peridots come from Zabargad and Myanmar, but Arizona, Hawaii, and Norway have also supplied fine gems.

VOLCANIC BOMB
This solidified lava contains fragments of rock rich in olivine. The lava came from deep within the earth, carrying the rock with it, and the whole piece was ejected through a volcano as a volcanic bomb.

ISLAND GEM
Peridot usually occurs in rocks intergrown with other minerals. The island of Zabargad in the Red Sea is one of the few places in the world where crystals with distinct faces, such as these, are found.

NAME CHANGE
There have been peridot mines on the island of Zabargad in the Red Sea for a long time. The stones from here were known by the ancient Greeks as *topazos* (pp. 112–113).

Moonstone

Moonstone is the best-known feldspar gem. Feldspars are common in rocks, but rarely of gem quality. There are two main groups: one which is rich in potash and includes the moonstones; one which is rich in soda and calcium and includes sunstone. They range in hardness from 6–6.5 and in specific gravity from 2.56–2.76.

SUNSTONE
The bright spangles in sunstones are reflections from tiny dark-red flakes of hematite. Some are arranged parallel, giving extra brightness in some directions.

The sun and the moon – appropriate names for these two stones

BLUISH MOON
Most moonstones are colorless with a silvery or bluish sheen, but some varieties may be steely gray, orange pink, yellow, or pale green. The gray stones particularly may show good cat's-eyes (pp. 102–103).

Pin set with sunstone

MOONSTONE
This large specimen of pegmatitic feldspar from Myanmar shows the moonstone sheen. Pegmatites (pp. 94–95) may also be the source of moonstones sometimes found in the gem gravels of Sri Lanka and India.

Ring set with moonstone

Continued on next page

Spinel

The most beautiful red and blue spinels can rival ruby and sapphire in their richness. Until the 19th century, red spinels were called balas rubies, which led to some confusion. The scientist Romé de l'Isle (pp. 82–83) was the first to distinguish clearly between true ruby and red spinel. The term *balas* may relate to a source of these stones in Balascia, now called Badakhshan, in Afghanistan.

PRINCELY REWARD
The Black Prince, son of King Edward III of England, helped Pedro the Cruel, King of Castile, Spain, to win the Battle of Najera in 1367. He was rewarded with a balas ruby, now in the British imperial state crown.

SPINEL CRYSTAL
Crystal system: cubic; hardness: 8; specific gravity: 3.5–3.7.

SMALL DISTORTION
Spinel usually crystallizes as octahedra. This specimen is a crystal aggregate (p. 93) of small distorted octahedra in parallel growth. Spinel often occurs as twins (p. 91), and when flat, such crystals are called macles.

POLISHED OVER
This crystal has been polished to remove surface blemishes, but it still has its original octahedral (eight-faced) shape.

Black Prince's ruby

Cullinan II diamond

REFORMED CHARACTER
This specimen from Lake Baikal, USSR, contains octahedra of blue spinel set in a matrix, or network, of white calcite and shiny muscovite mica. Originally it was probably an impure limestone which completely recrystallized under moderate temperature and pressure.

LYING IN STATE
The Black Prince's ruby in the British imperial state crown is really a 170-carat spinel, once called a ballas ruby. It is mounted above another famous stone, the Cullinan II diamond (p. 105). The Timur ruby, which belongs to England's Queen Elizabeth II, is also a spinel.

CLOSE TO HOME
Most gem spinels are recovered from gravels in Sri Lanka and Myanmar. These Myanmar fragments are not very worn, indicating that they have not traveled far from their source.

THORNY CRYSTALS
These beautifully crystallized octahedra from Bodenmais in Germany are gahnite, a zinc-rich variety of spinel. They show the typical triangular-shaped crystal faces of spinel which may account for the possible derivation of its name from the Latin *spina*, meaning thorn.

CRYSTAL COLORS
Pure spinel is colorless. The beautiful reds and pinks are due to small amounts of chromium in the crystals. Blues and greens are caused by iron and, rarely, by zinc.

Zircon

The name zircon comes from the Arabic *zargoon*, meaning vermilion or golden-colored. Sri Lanka has been a source of zircons for 2,000 years, but today stones also come from Thailand, Australia, and Brazil. Colorless zircon looks like diamond in luster and fire and is used as a diamond simulant (p. 97), but it is softer and may look "sleepy" due to inclusions (p. 91) and double refraction (p. 89).

The color of red hyacinths may account for red zircon once being known as hyacinth

NATURAL COLORS
Zircon is zirconium silicate, colorless when pure, but found in a wide range of colors in nature because of different impurities.

ZIRCON CRYSTAL
Crystal system: tetragonal; hardness: 6–7.5; specific gravity: 4.6–4.7.

RADIOACTIVE
This exceptionally large pebble from Sri Lankan gem gravels shows a typical zircon color. Some zircons contain so much uranium and thorium that the radioactivity of these elements breaks down the crystal structure and the stone becomes amorphous, or noncrystalline.

HEAT TREATMENT
Colorless, blue, and golden zircons can be produced by heating red-brown crystals. Heating in an oxygen-free atmosphere produces blue zircon; heating in air, i.e. with oxygen, produces a golden color. Some colorless stones are produced by both methods. These colors may fade but can be restored by reheating.

Natural brown zircon crystals

Heat-treated blue zircon crystals

Stones cut from heat-treated zircon

Chrysoberyl

Gem chrysoberyl is exceeded in hardness only by diamond and corundum. The yellow, green, and brown colors are caused by iron and chromium. There are three varieties: clear yellow-green gems; cat's-eye, or cymophane, usually cut as cabochons to display the "eye" effect (p. 103); and alexandrite, famous for its dramatic color change. Sri Lanka and Brazil are sources for all three, but the best alexandrites come from the USSR.

ALEXANDRITE
Alexandrite was discovered in the Ural Mountains, USSR, on the birthday of Czar Alexander II in 1830, hence the name. They appear a deep green in daylight and red in artificial light, matching the Russian imperial colors.

Cut yellow chrysoberyl

Cut alexandrite

POPULAR IN PORTUGAL
Yellow-green chrysoberyls were found in Brazil in the 18th century. These became very popular in Portuguese and Spanish jewelry.

CHRYSOBERYL CRYSTAL
Crystal system: orthorhombic; hardness: 8.5; specific gravity: 3.68–3.78.

Collectors' items

WITH OVER 3,000 SPECIES OF MINERAL to choose from, the potential number of gems would appear at first to be very large. But crucial factors such as hardness (pp. 88–89), durability, and rarity reduce the number of commercial gems to a few dozen. Many people collect rarities that are not in general circulation. They may seek the rare colors or exceptional sizes of common gems, or cut examples of minerals too soft or fragile to wear in jewelry. For example, blende and sphene are available in reasonable quantities but are too soft for constant wear. Benitoite is durable enough to be worn but is too rare to be generally available.

AXINITE
The most beautiful wedge-shaped crystals of brown axinite come from Bourg d'Oisans in France and display flashes of gray and violet in different directions. Although they were once extremely rare, crystals are being recovered more regularly from the Sri Lanka gem gravels.

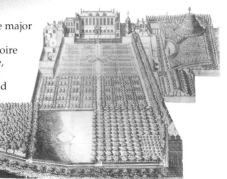

SPHENE
Ranging from golden yellow brown to bright emerald green, sphene has great luster and fire but is too soft for general wear. The finest gems come from the Austrian and Swiss Alps, Myanmar, and California.

FRENCH COLLECTION
The first specimens of the major mineral collection in the Muséum National d'Histoire Naturelle in Paris, France, were brought together in Louis XIII's pharmacy and botanical gardens. This engraving shows the gardens as they were in 1636, seven years before the king died.

ALPINE EXPERTS
Many fine crystals are collected from crystal-lined clefts in the Alps by people known as *strahlern*. *Strahlern* are experienced mountaineers but also talented mineral collectors, usually with great knowledge of a particular Alpine area.

TANZANITE
The purplish blue gem variety of the mineral zoisite is tanzanite. It was found in northern Tanzania in 1967 and is remarkable for its displays of rich blue, magenta, and yellowish gray. Many crystals are greenish gray and are heat-treated to the more attractive blue.

DANBURITE
The mineral danburite is named after Danbury, Connecticut, where it was first found as colorless crystals in a pegmatite (p. 95). Fine yellow stones come from Madagascar and Myanmar, and colorless stones from Japan and Mexico.

CORDIERITE
Fine, gem-quality cordierite comes from Sri Lanka, Myanmar, Madagascar, and India. Cordierite is exceptional in showing very strong pleochroism (pp. 106–107), from deep purplish blue in one direction, to pale yellowish gray in another. This pleochroism was used by the Vikings for navigating their long boats and has also led to the crystals being called water sapphires.

BENITOITE

The color of benitoite crystals can be compared with that of fine sapphires (pp. 106–107). They display similar fire to diamonds (pp. 104–105), but remain collectors' stones because of their rarity. Benitoite comes from localities in San Benito County, California, after which it is named (pp. 80–81).

The San Benito mine in 1914 showing the open cut and an ore bucket on the left

BLENDE

The popular name for sphalerite, the world's major source of zinc, is blende. Normally it is opaque gray to black, but gem-quality reddish brown, yellow, and green crystals come from Mexico and Spain. The rich colors are very attractive, but the stones are too soft to be used in jewelry.

Blende crystals in matrix

Rough blende crystal

Kunzite crystal

Cut pale-green spodumene

Cut kunzite

SPODUMENE

Magnificent crystals of spodumene come from Brazil, California, and Afghanistan. Fine gems weighing hundreds of carats have been cut from pale-green and yellow crystals, and from the pink variety kunzite, named after G. F. Kunz. Small crystals of a rare, emerald-green variety called hiddenite are found in North Carolina and Sri Lanka.

George Frederick Kunz, an author on gems, who worked for the New York jewelers Tiffany's early this century

GOLDNEY GROTTO

Precious stones and corals are among items collected to cover the walls and pillars of this underground grotto. It was built between 1737 and 1764 near Bristol, England.

SCAPOLITE

Myanmar and East Africa are sources of scapolite gems. They occur in pastel shades of yellow, pink, purple, and fine cat's-eyes (p. 102–103).

SINHALITE

Originally traded as peridot from Sri Lanka, sinhalite was proved in 1952 to be a new species. Mineralogists in the British Museum named it after an old name for Sri Lanka – Sinhala.

FIBROLITE

This bluish violet stone of 19.84 carats is fibrolite, a rare variety of the mineral sillimanite. It comes from Myanmar and is one of the largest in the world. Andalusite has the same chemical composition – aluminum silicate – but a different structure. The gem-quality stones show bold red and green pleochroic colors. Fine examples come from Brazil and Sri Lanka.

Cut fibrolite

Cut andalusite

Stones for carving

MICROCRYSTALLINE ROCKS and minerals have been used in decoration for thousands of years. The best known are the jades, lapis lazuli, and turquoise, and there are many more which are suitable for carving work. Ancient civilizations such as the Egyptians, Chinese, and Sumerians used jade, lapis, and turquoise to make jewelry. South American Indians and the Maoris of New Zealand have been carving turquoise and jade for centuries.

TURQUOISE TRADITION
Traditional Indian jewelry has been made for thousands of years in the southwestern USA, where most turquoise is still produced.

MALACHITE
Malachite is a vivid green copper mineral. It is often found as kidney-shaped masses surrounded by bands of color. It is 4 on the hardnes scale (pp. 88–89) and has a specific gravity of 3.8. Zaire, Zambia, Australia, and the USSR are the main sources.

Lapis lazuli

Lapis lazuli is not a single mineral but a rock consisting of blue lazurite with variable amounts of calcite and pyrite. The best, from Afghanistan, consists mostly of lazurite and is deep blue. It is 5.5 on Mohs' hardness scale and has a specific gravity of 2.7–2.9. There are other sources in the Soviet Union and Chile.

White calcite

PERSIAN BLUE
The name lapis lazuli is derived from the Persian word *lazhward,* meaning blue. The blue color is caused by sulfur which is an essential part of its composition.

Turquoise

The word *turquoise* comes from the French *pierre turquoise,* meaning stone of Turkey; in the past most turquoise was sold in Turkey. It occurs in nodules and veins of green or blue. Copper makes it blue; iron makes it green. It has a specific gravity of 2.6–2.9 and a hardness of 5–6.

NATURAL MOSAIC
Turquoise is rare in large masses and is more often found forming mosaics. The finest blue turquoise comes from Iran (previously called Persia), where it has been used in decoration for almost 6,000 years.

POPULAR JEWEL
Lapis lazuli has been used extensively for beads and other pieces of jewelry.

MEDIEVAL PAINTING
In medieval times lapis lazuli was crushed and purified to make the paint pigment ultramarine. It was used to paint the Wilton Diptych, a detail of which is shown here. This famous altarpiece is now in the National Gallery in London, England.

Blue Persian turquoise engraved and inlaid with gold

ANCIENT SKULL
This mask, shaped around a human skull, was made by the Aztecs, an ancient civilization of Central America. It is made of turquoise and lignum, and may represent Tezcatlipoca, an important Aztec god.

Jade

The Spanish conquerors of Mexico believed that the Indians' green stones would cure kidney ailments. They called them kidney stones or *piedras de hijadas* and from this the word *jade* was derived. In Europe, the name was then given to material of the same color and hardness which was imported from China. It was only in 1863 that they were proved to be two different minerals now called jadeite and nephrite.

JADEITE
The major source of jadeite is Myanmar. It varies widely in color so a window is cut in stones for sale to show the color. The most prized color is the emerald-green jadeite known as imperial jade. Jadeite has a hardness of 6.5–7 and a specific gravity of 3.3–3.5.

Jadeite fashioned into a ball

LIFE JACKET
The ancient Chinese believed that jade had the power to give life and used it to try to preserve the dead. They linked plates of nephrite around the corpse to make a funeral suit. This one belonged to a princess of the 2nd century B.C. and is linked with gold.

Nephrite snail designed by the famous Russian jeweler Fabergé

CHINESE CAMEL
This nephrite camel was carved in China. White and cream nephrites contain very little iron. More iron causes the spinach-green stones of the USSR, Canada, and New Zealand and the black jade of South Australia.

NEPHRITE
Nephrite is made of interlocking grains, making the stone tough. The "greenstone" used by the Maoris of New Zealand is nephrite. It has a hardness of 6.5 and a specific gravity of 2.9–3.1.

RHODONITE
The bright pink color of rhodonite (*rhodo* means pink) is caused by manganese. It has a hardness of about 6 and is used for carving and inlays. Sources of gem material include USSR, Canada, and Australia.

Other stones

Many other stones are popular for carving, mainly because of their color. These include malachite, serpentine, blue john, and rhodonite as well as marbles and alabaster.

SERPENTINE
The patterns in serpentine often look like snake-skin, and carvers can use these to create works of art. Some is soft and easy to carve, but the yellow-green variety bowenite, a favorite of Chinese carvers, is harder – up to 6 on Mohs' scale.

BLUE JOHN
The distinctive purple and pale yellow banded fluorite called blue john comes from Derbyshire in England. It is fragile, so is usually bonded with resins to make it easier to work and harder-wearing.

19th-century blue john vase

121

Animal and vegetable

GEMS DERIVED FROM ANIMALS AND PLANTS are described as organic. They include amber, jet, coral, pearl, and shell. They are not as hard (4 or less) or as dense (1.04 – amber; 2.78 – pearl) as gemstones but have been popular for thousands of years because of their beauty. Beads of shell and amber have been found in ancient graves dating from 2000 B.C. Pearls have long had great value as symbols of beauty and purity. The Roman emperor Julius Caesar is said to have paid the equivalent of about $250,000 for a single pearl.

PREHISTORIC GEMS
In the Jurassic period, 160 million years ago, dinosaurs and other giant reptiles lived among the trees, which produced amber and jet.

Jet and amber

Jet and amber both come from trees. Jet is a fine-grained black rock formed over millions of years from rotted and compressed trees, in a similar way to coal. Amber is the fossilized resin, or sap, of trees that lived as much as 300 million years ago.

JET-LAGGED
This piece of jet shows its origin. It contains fossils of several long-extinct animals, including an ammonite. Unlike coal, it is hard-wearing and can be polished.

Fossil ammonite

ANCIENT TRAVELER
The major source of amber is the south and east coast of the Baltic Sea. Amber is only slightly denser than seawater, and large lumps can be carried long distances across the sea. This specimen was found on the east coast of England.

Coral

Coral is a skeleton of calcium carbonate made by colonies of soft-bodied animals which live in tropical or subtropical waters. The range of colors, from black to blue to cream to red, is due to different growth conditions and organic contents.

Carving from Mediterranean coral of a monkey clinging to a branch

Coral living in a tropical sea

ANCIENT VALUES
These branches of the highly prized red coral are from the Mediterranean species *Corallium rubrum*. It was greatly valued by the ancient Romans.

NECKLACE MATERIAL
This blue coral comes from the species *Heliopora caerulea* which grows in the seas around the Philippines. It is often cut into beads for necklaces.

Pearl and shell

The sheen on pearls and the inside of some shells is caused by light reflecting on tiny plates of calcium carbonate called nacre. Pearls, found in some marine and freshwater shells, form when a foreign body such as a sand grain becomes lodged inside the shell. To stop the irritation, the animal slowly surrounds the grains with nacre.

OYSTER CATCHERS
For more than 2,000 years the Persian Gulf has supplied the most beautiful natural pearls. The oysters (*Pinctada vulgaris*) used to be recovered by teams of divers. Today many pearls are cultured. An irritant is put into the oysters and the shells are farmed for their pearls.

PEARLS OF COLOR
Pearls come in many colors including blackish, golden yellow, pink, cream, and white.

MAXIMUM SIZE
The best pearls come from oysters and mussels. *Pinctada maxima* is the largest pearl oyster. It is found in the seas around Australia and Malaysia.

Mother-of-pearl

BUNCH OF PEARLS
Bombay, India, has been a center of pearl drilling for centuries. Some were sold as a "Bombay bunch." Each size was strung separately on silk, then combined with strings of other sizes suitable for a necklace, and finished off with tassels of silver wire.

Iridescent nacre

CANNING JEWEL
Irregularly shaped pearls are called baroque pearls. There are four, including a magnificent one forming the body, in the Canning Triton jewel. It was probably made in south Germany in the late 16th century and is now in the Victoria and Albert Museum in London.

Baroque pearl

SHELL SHINE
Shells with brightly colored blue and green nacre belong to the genus *Haliotis*. They are found in American waters, where they are called abalone, and in the seas around New Zealand, where they are called paua.

Pillbox with an abalone lid

Crystals at home

M ANY EVERYDAY OBJECTS in the home are crystalline. There are ice crystals in the freezer, salt and sugar crystals in the food cupboard and in food itself, crystals of vitamin C and aspirin in the medicine cabinet, tartrate crystals in the wine bottle, and silicon crystal chips in the refrigerator and washing machine. The TV, telephone, radio, and camera work because of crystals, the house is built of materials which are mostly crystalline, and outside, bikes and cars stand slowly rusting – crystallizing!

BY A WHISKER

"Hello. This is New York. Here is the news." This might be what these women are listening to using a crystal set. In this early form of radio, operators moved a thin copper wire, sometimes known as a cat's whisker, against a galena crystal to pick up radio waves. Crystal sets became popular in the 1920s when public broadcasting began.

FOR THE RECORD

In some record players, there are two crystals. The stylus is made of hard-wearing diamond or corundum, and a piezoelectric crystal (p. 101) in the cartridge converts vibrations received from the record into an electric charge.

Diamond stylus

Enlarged photograph of a diamond stylus traveling through the groove on a stereo record

SPOONFUL OF SUGAR

Over 100 million tons of sugar are crystallized every year in refineries. Sugar is extracted as a liquid solution from raw sugar cane or beet, then converted into sugar crystals. The silver spoon holding these sugar crystals is itself a mass of silver crystals.

Liquid crystal display

Greatly enlarged photograph of crystals of vitamin C

CRYSTAL DISPLAY

The displays in many calculators are liquid crystal displays (LCDs). Liquid crystals are not truly crystalline. They flow like a liquid but have molecules arranged like those of crystals and some properties of crystals. Power rearranges the molecules so that they reflect or absorb light and show dark or light.

VITAL INTAKE

These tablets contain crystals of ascorbic acid, or vitamin C. Ascorbic acid is a white crystalline substance present in plants, especially citrus fruits, tomatoes, and green vegetables. Vitamins are essential to us in small quantities. Most cannot be produced by the body, and therefore have to be taken in through food or tablets.

PRECIOUS STONES
Many people own jewelry made with precious or semiprecious stones. This silver brooch contains diamonds, a blue sapphire, and a pearl.

Photo enlargement of needle-like crystals in kettle "fur"

KETTLE FUR
Crystals can be found in your kettle. Even after purification processes there are still some harmless minerals dissolved in tap water. These crystallize and coat the inside of your kettle when the water is boiled.

ON FILM
When a photograph is taken, an image is recorded on light-sensitive material by the action of light. Most film uses light-sensitive crystals of silver salts. The photographic industry is one of the largest users of silver.

Photo enlargement of silver nitrate crystals on a photographic film

Hand lens for studying the major features of crystals

PRESSED FOR TIME
Many watches use tiny quartz crystals to control time (p. 100–101), and ruby is used for watch bearings. The ruby crystals are usually synthetic (pp. 96–97).

Ruby crystals

Collecting

Crystal collecting can be enjoyed without spending too much money. Crystals can be collected in the field, bought, or exchanged with friends and dealers. They are usually fragile and should be carefully stored. Those found in the field should be kept with details of where they were found and, if possible, their host rock.

Wulfenite crystal

IN MINIATURE
A popular method of collecting and storing crystals is as "micromount" specimens a few millimeters in size. They take up little space, and fine crystal groups of rare and unusual minerals can be collected.

Amethyst crystals

CAVITY FILLERS
Crystal-lined geodes are often found within basaltic lava flows. They are formed from fluids which filter through the rocks and crystallize in available cavities. They may be highly prized by collectors.

FIELDWORK
Use a geological hammer to collect in the field. Wear suitable clothing and boots, a hard hat, and eye protector. Ask permission to collect on private land and always observe the local laws.

Index

Acknowledgments

DK would like to thank:

For their invaluable assistance during photography, providing specimens and specialist information:
Dr. Wendy Kirk of University College London; the staff of the Natural History Museum, especially Peter Tandy; Gavin Morgan, Nick Merryman, and Christine Jones at the Museum of London; Redland Brick Company and Jacobson Hirsch for the loan of equipment; Plymouth Marine Laboratory; the National Museum of Wales; Kew Gardens; De Beers Industrial Diamond Division for the loan of diamond tools (p. 99); Keith Hammond for the loan of the beryl crystal (p. 91); Nancy Armstrong for the loan of the prospector's brooch (p. 111); and Meryl Silbert.

Lester Cheeseman, Tim Hammond, Thomas Keenes, Anna Kunst, and David Nixon for their editorial and design assistance, and Anne-Marie Bulat for her work on the intitial stages of the book.

Paul Taylor would like to thank: M.K. Howarth, C. Patterson, R.A. Fortey, C.H.C. Brunton, A.W. Gentry, B.R. Rosen, J.B. Richardson, P.L. Forey, N.J. Morris, C.B. Stringer, A.B. Smith, J.E.P. Whittaker, R. Croucher, S.F. Morris, C.R. Hill, A.C. Milner, R.L. Hodgkinson, C.A. Walker, R.J. Cleevely, C.H. Shute, V.T. Young, D.N. Lewis, A.E. Longbottom, M. Crawley, R. Kruszynski, C. Bell, S.C. Naylor, A. Lum, R.W. Ingle, P.D. Jenkins, P.D. Hillyard, D.T. Moore, J.W. Schopf, C.M. Butler, P.W. Jackson.

Additional photography: Karl Shone (pp. 98–99, 124–125).

Artwork: John Woodcock; Eugene Fleury; Ray Owen; Nick Madren; Fred Ford and Mike Pilley of Radius Graphics; Thomas Keenes; and Andrew Macdonald (48cl, 52bl, 56cl).

Indexers: Marion Dent and Jane Parker.

Editorial Coordinator: Marion Dent
Editor: Julie Ferris
Designers: Emma Bowden, Joanne Connor

Picture credits
(l =left r=right t=top b=below c=center a=above)

Peter Amacher: 118cl.
Alison Anholt-White: 20tl.
Ancient Art and Architecture Collection: 79cl.
Archives Pierrre et Marie Curie: 101bc.
Ardea: 9bl, 13c, 34c, 34bl, 35t.
Aspect Picture Library / Geoff Tompkinson: 98br.
Dr. Peter Bancroft: 115cr.
Bergakademie Freiberg: 82cl, 89br.
Bibliotheca Ambrosiana, Milan: 83cr.
Bibliotheque St. Die: 73cl.
Biofotos / Heather Angel: 18c, 23cr, 31br, 36–37bc.
Bridgeman Art Library: 10cr, 72tr, 88tl; / Christie's, London: 97br; / Bibliotheque Nationale, Paris: 112tr.
Paul Brierley: 69b, 86cr.
F. Brisse, "La Symetrie Bidimensionnelle et le Canada," Canadian Mineralogist, 19, 217–224 (1981): 83tc.
British Geological Survey: 125br.
Gordon Bussey: 124tl.
Californian Division of Mines and Geology: 119tl.
Dept. of Earth Sciences, University of Cambridge: 31cr.
Bruce Coleman: 14c; / Jeff Foote 20tr, 31c, 32c; / Michael Freeman 72c.
Lawrence H. Conklin: 119bl.
Simon Conway Morris: 12c.
Crown Copyright: 73tl, 116cr.
De Beers: 99bl, 99tc, 104cr, 105br.
Diamond Information Centre: 74c.
C.M. Dixon / Photoresources: 48t, 49t, 53b.
Dorling Kindersley / Eric Crichton: 117tc.
Drukker International BV, Amsterdam: 98tr.
e.t. archive: 111br.
Mary Evans Picture Library: 7cl, 10br, 11tl, 12c, 40t, 44, 45c, 46b, 49b, 50tl, 53t, 59, 60b, 62t, 62cl, 64t, 65t, 70cr, 71c, 77tr, 85tl, 93br, 94cl, 108–109c, 108bl, 116tr.

Vivien Fifield: 42bl.
Fondation M.S.A.: 81tl; / A. Bucher: 100tl.
Michael Freeman: 95tc, 107c.
Geological Society: 38t.
Geoscience Features Picture Library: 9tr, 43tl, 43tc, 43tr, 52t.
David George: 17c.
Robert Harding Picture Library: 13br, 21c, 47c, 52br, 55, 56bl, 57c, 61t, 61b, 63t, 63b, 70t, 114tr, 121tl; / N.A. Callow: 47b; / G&P Corrigan: 57t; / Jon Gardey: 64b; / Ian Griffiths: 47t; / Brian Hawkes: 46c; / Walter Rawlings: 60c; / A.C. Waltham 56br.
Harvard Mineralogical Museum: 90cl.
Ernst A. Heiniger: 109br.
Michael Holford: 6tl, 77cl, 107br, 114cr, 120br.
Glenn I. Huss: 64c.
The Hutchison Library: 16tl, 63c, 70cl.
Image Bank / Lynn M. Stone: 103cr. / Lionel ASY-Schwart: 122bl.
India Office: 106tr.
Kobal Collection: 105cr.
Kodak Ltd.: 125c.
Kuntshistoriches Museum, Vienna / Photo: Courtauld Institute of Art: 110tr.
Lauros-Giraudon: 104bl. Mansell Collection: 18t, 32b, 85bl, 105cl, 115c, 122tr.
Moebius / Exhibition Bijoux Cailloux Fous, Strasbourg: 80bc.
Museum of London: 75tl, 75br.
Museum National d'Histoire Naturelle, Paris: 118cr.
Museum of Mankind 72bl.
NASA: 65br.
National Gallery: 120bl.
National Portrait Gallery, London: 113tr.
Natural History Museum: 66c, 67, 85tr, 89tr, 89c, 103br, 110bc, 121br; / Frank Greenaway FRPS: 81bl, 91bc; / P. Krishna, S.S. Jiang, and A.R. Lang: 91tc; / Harry Taylor ABIPP: 101br.
Northern Ireland Tourist Board: 92bl.
Oxford Scientific Films: 36bl.
Perham's of West Paris, Maine: 93tr.
Phototake, NYC / Yoav Levy: 100cr.
Planet Earth Pictures: 24cl, 33c, 35cl, 36cr.
Katrina Raphaell: 101cr.
Ann Ronan Picture Library: 11tc, 42br, 97tc, 97cr, 123tc.
Royal Geographical Society: 106bl, 109tc.
S. Australian Dept. of Mines and Energy / B. Sowry: 111tc.
Science Photo Library: 79tr, 84bl; / Dr. Jeremy Burgess: 76tr, 124c, 125tr; / ESA / PLI: 78tl; / John Howard: 113cr; / Peter Menzel: 95c; / NASA: 96c; / David Parker: 79br; / Soames Summerhays: 78bl.
Smithsonian Institution: 107tr, 109t, 112br.
Brian Stevenson & Co: 95bl.
Stockphotos: 90br.
R.F. Symes: 45tr, 90tr.
Syndication International: 86c, 120tr.
Uffizi, Florence / Photo: Giraudon: 102cl.
University College London / Mike Gray: 51, 54tr, 58tr.
Victoria and Albert Museum: 121cr, 123bl.
Werner Forman Archive: 75c.
Peter Woloszynski: 119cr.
Woodmansterne: / Clive Friend: 49c; / Nicholas Servian: 62cr.
ZEFA: 12–13bl, 50tr; / Leidmann: 102tr.
Zeiss: 65bl.

Every effort has been made to trace the copyright holders of photographs. The publishers apologize for any omissions and will amend future editions.